TAMING THE MONEY MONSTER

FOCUS ON THE FAMILY
RESOURCES

TAMING THE MONEY MONSTER

RON BLUE

FIVE STEPS TO CONQUERING DEBT

TYNDALE

TAMING THE MONEY MONSTER
Copyright © 1989, 1993 by Ron Blue
Library of Congress Cataloging-in-Publication Data
Blue, Ron, 1942-
    Taming the money monster: five steps to conquering debt / Ron Blu
        p. cm.
    ISBN 1-56179-587-9
    1. Finance, Personal 2. Saving and investment 3. Debt I. Title.
    HG179.B5657 1989 1993
    332.024'02-dc20   93-105.63
                                                         CIP

A Focus on the Family book published by
Tyndale House Publishers, Wheaton, Illinois 60189

TYNDALE is a registered trademark of Tyndale House Publishers, In
Tyndale's quill logo is a trademark of Tyndale House Publishers, Inc.

Unless otherwise noted, Scripture quotations are from The New King
James Version, copyright © 1979, 1980, 1982 by Thomas Nelson, Inc.,
Publisher. Quotations identified NIV are from the Holy Bible, New
International Version, copyright © 1973, 1978, 1984 by the Internatior
Bible Society.

Certain details of case studies mentioned in this book have been
changed to protect the privacy of the people involved.

This book is a revised and updated edition of The Debt Squeeze.
Excerpt from Ladies' Home Journal, © copyright 1986, Meredith
Corporation. All rights reserved. Reprinted with permission.
Appendix A taken from Closer Walk magazine, copyright © 1989,
Walk Thru the Bible Ministries, Atlanta, Georgia. Used by
permission. Excerpts from Money magazine used by permission.
Chart 11.4 used by permission of Runzheimer International.

Editor: Larry K. Weeden
Cover design: Imagestudios

Printed in the United States of America
05 06 07 08 09/10 9 8 7 6 5 4

To my wife, Judy,
who has kept me, through wise counsel,
from making many foolish debt decisions;
and to my Lord and Savior, Jesus Christ,
to whom I am eternally indebted

Contents

Acknowledgments

There are many to whom I owe a debt of gratitude for assistance with this book. No book can ever be written by one individual. Not only was there the administrative and technical help in putting together a book, but also those who offered advice and encouragement during the writing process.

By far the most significant contributor to this work was my wife, Judy. She typed the entire manuscript many times as we went through the revisions. This was an especially enjoyable project for the two of us as we talked about the issues raised herein. Judy has been more than I could have hoped for in a wife and mother to our children.

The second acknowledgment must go to Dr. James Dobson and his team. The more I've come to know him and his leadership staff over the years, the more impressed I am with the integrity and impact of their ministry. It gives me great joy to participate jointly with them in the outreach of this book. A special note of thanks must go to Rolf Zettersten for his initial enthusiasm, Rick Christian for his continual encouragement throughout the writing process, and Larry Weeden, who served as a kind but firm editor.

Zoe Custer, my faithful assistant during this process, had to endure the frequent scheduling changes caused by the time requirements of writing. She did so, as usual, with great patience. Kelly Pierce assisted greatly in the development of many of the charts. Blair Cunningham and Curt Knorr helped with the technical analysis. Horace Holley, a good friend who has committed his life to debt counseling, gave me good advice, especially about those who have severe debt problems.

Finally, the whole staff at Ronald Blue & Co. has been extraordinarily patient with me during the writing of this book. To them I offer sincere thanks.

CHAPTER ONE

Taming the Money Monster

A friend recently completed an intensive, one-month course leading to being licensed to drive an 18-wheeler. At the end of the course, each candidate was quizzed by a panel of experienced drivers. The questions were grueling. The last was stated this way: "We are going to describe a specific driving situation, and we want your specific response about what you would do.

"Here's the situation. You are driving your fully loaded 18-wheeler down a mountain road. To your right is a 300-foot wall going straight up. To your left is a 1,000-foot drop-off. There is no guardrail, and the berm is narrow and covered with gravel. Immediately in front of you is a fully loaded logging truck traveling very slowly.

"As you pull out to pass, you see a fearful sight. Another 18-wheeler is rounding a curve—coming up the road directly at you. At that instant, a car pulls out to pass the truck coming

3

up the road. You apply your brakes and get no response. Your brakes have failed. Four vehicles are now coming together at the same place at the same time. Our question is, what specifically are you going to do?"

My friend thought for a few moments and then answered, "I guess I'll wake up Leroy."

The panel was perplexed, and one of the questioners said, "Who's Leroy?"

My friend responded, "Leroy's my relief driver, and he's been sleeping back in the sleeper."

Now the panel was really confused. One of them asked, "How is waking up your relief driver going to help in any way?"

"It's not really going to help," said my friend, "but, you see, Leroy's from a little town in north Georgia, and he's never seen a wreck like this one's going to be!"

Obviously, that's not a true story. It's a joke that a friend of mine, Colonel Nimrod McNair, has been telling for as long as I've known him. But I believe it illustrates well how many of us feel—that we're living in economic times when the brakes have failed and we're out of control. Unless something happens soon, there's going to be an accident such as we've never seen.

In the last 12 years, the national debt has increased fourfold to over $4 trillion. It's now growing at the rate of $13,000 per second. In Larry Burkett's recent best-seller *The Coming Economic Earthquake*, he explained clearly what's likely to happen because our national debt is out of control.

I just finished reading another book titled *Bankruptcy 1995*. Its authors predict that the United States will be unable to pay its bills by 1995. They also believe we're beyond the point of no return and that it's now impossible to stem the tide of debt and forestall a national bankruptcy.

Japan and Europe have replaced the United States as the dominant players in the world's economy. The U.S., which at the end of World War II controlled over two-thirds of the world's investable assets, now controls less than one-third.

AN INDIVIDUAL PROBLEM, TOO

Unfortunately, it isn't just the federal government that's up to its ears in debt. Individuals and families are, too. Personal credit card debt in the U.S. reached $247 billion by the end of 1992. In addition to that, consumers owed $720 billion of installment debt. All told, American families owe nearly $1 trillion in consumer debt—for items they bought that have lost most of their value and are rapidly losing what's left. Consumer debt amounts to 16.1 percent of personal disposable income. In other words, if an average family decided to pay off all its consumer debt, it would take 16 percent of next year's income to do so.

When that much of a family's income is committed to debt repayment, not much is left for other priorities. Saving for things like replacement of cars and appliances, emergencies, college education for the kids, and retirement for the parents is next to impossible. As a result, most families live from paycheck to paycheck, and they're just one payday away from financial ruin. Their future doesn't look much brighter, either.

I could go on, further depressing you with facts you probably know only too well. But the real issue is the same one posed by the panel of questioners to Leroy's partner: "So what specifically are you going to do?" To put it another way, "How are you going to tame your personal money monster?"

REASON FOR HOPE

Despite the gloomy statistics, I believe there's good reason for hope. No matter what your specific situation, you can be excited and encouraged. Why? Because in times of financial uncertainty, those who follow biblical principles of money management will not only survive, but even prosper. God's truths are timeless, and He has some definite things to say that are right on target in today's uncertain economic environment.

To illustrate the struggles caused by debt and the positive steps anyone can take to deal with it, I'm going to introduce three sets of people in three different situations. My hope is that you'll be able to relate to one or more of their stories. Then, in the chapters that follow, we'll look at the things they and you can do to throw a net over the money monster.

Tom and Sue are a typical middle-aged, middle-class couple. There's nothing extravagant about their life-style, but they own a home and two cars and live comfortably. Early in their marriage, they got in the habit of buying what they wanted right away with credit cards or installment loans. As a result, they have overspent their income by just a little year after year.

Now Tom and Sue find themselves $7,000 in debt, with no savings, no money set aside toward their children's college education, and both cars in need of replacement before long. They realize they need to change their habits before it's too late.

Betty is a single mom with two children. Her former husband left her after running up debt on four credit cards. Because of the way our laws work, she is liable for those debts. Out of her monthly take-home pay of approximately $1,200, she tithes and pays rent, utilities, groceries, and so on. Her budget leaves no room for doctors, prescriptions, clothes, entertainment, or car repairs.

Like many divorced mothers, Betty receives no child support. Her former husband is over $25,000 in arrears and will probably never make that up, let alone start to make regular payments.

Betty feels the local school is too dangerous

for her children, so she has placed them, at great cost, in a private Christian school. That school has been patient with her and is helping her as much as it can, but she continues to fall further behind. She now owes $2,900 on credit cards and $1,000 to the Christian school. She isn't pay-· ing anything on two of the credit card balances, and she pays $35 a month on the other two. At her current rate of repayment, she will never be free of any of those debts.

As you might imagine, Betty is not too worried about the national debt, or even about what happens to tax rates. She's concerned about how to put food on the table and make next month's payments.

Phil and Jenny are among the thousands of couples who started their own small business in recent years. Unfortunately, however, their efforts ended in business and personal bankruptcy (largely because of legal problems with a former partner). Although that freed them lawfully from the business's huge debts, they were left owing $13,000 to their lawyer and $12,000 to Jenny's parents for help received while they were still trying to keep the company afloat. The IRS also claims they owe back payroll taxes from their failed business.

Determined to make a fresh start, Phil and Jenny moved halfway across the country. They now have no access to credit and must pay cash for everything. Both hold down full-time jobs, but they dream of starting another business with growth potential so Jenny can stay home with their young children even as they continue to repay their debts.

DO WHAT ONLY YOU CAN DO

As you consider the potential economic catastrophe confronting all of us and your own struggles with your personal money monster, it will help to begin by asking yourself two questions. First, "What is the worst thing that can happen to you?" It could be the loss of a job, the death of a spouse, divorce, a medical emergency, or even a political or economic collapse such as what happened recently in Eastern Europe. Second, "Which of those potential events can you control?" The answer is, of course, none of them.

Being debt-free is your best preparation for an uncertain economic future.

In light of that reality, what *can* you do to get your finances under control and prepare yourself for an uncertain future? The answer, which may surprise you, is that you can do quite a lot. In fact, *only you can take the most important steps possible.*

Specifically, you can do five crucial things.

First, you can start by getting a complete, realistic picture of your current financial situation. (I'll explain how to do that in detail in chap. 7.) You have to know where you are before you can plan how to get where you want to be.

Second, you can begin to reduce and even eliminate all your debt. Being debt-free is your best preparation for an uncertain economic future.

Third, you can start to set aside money in a savings account for emergencies and major purchases. In effect, you become your own banker. Then, when it's time to buy a major appliance, car, or furniture, you take the money out of your savings and essentially borrow from yourself. If you have a periodic savings program, you can replace the money the same as if you were making installment or credit card payments. But now, instead of paying interest to someone else, you're rebuilding your savings and *earning* interest.

Fourth—and this depends on your doing the two preceding things—you can live within your income. Financial success does *not* depend on large investment returns or a growing income. Rather, it's as simple as spending less than you earn and doing it over a long period. If you take this step, you *will* be getting yourself out of debt, you *will* be saving, and you *will* be protecting yourself from our uncertain economic future. You'll never find yourself, as the U.S. finds itself today, living beyond your income and thereby approaching financial catastrophe.

Fifth, you can develop the correct perspective, remembering that God is the source of everything. The Lord said, "I will never leave you nor forsake you" (Heb. 13:5). The same verse urges us to "be content with such things as you have." The apostle Paul said, "I have learned in whatever state I am, to be content" (Phil. 4:11). Those statements provide tremendous financial wisdom.

If you have no debt, you're saving regularly, you're living within your income, and you're placing your trust in the living God—and then you lose your job or suffer some other catastrophe—you will have done all you can do. And in that case, I believe you will survive and even thrive.

IT CAN BE DONE
In 1982, I spoke at a conference and challenged the people to do two things: determine their long-term goals and pay off all their debt. One couple that heard me speak later asked me to help them develop a strategy to get out of debt and increase their charitable giving. They happened to live in Southern California, where the economy was booming.

Ten years later, I was at a Christmas party with that couple, and the man came up to me with tears in his eyes, gave me a hug, and said,

"I want to thank you for the counsel you gave us." During the 1980s, when Southern California was prospering, this couple methodically paid off their debts. Their friends considered them to be foolish because they weren't using borrowed money to get rich like so many other people. But when California's economy weakened almost to the point of depression, the story reversed. That couple then found themselves out of debt, with significant savings set aside for the future. In a time of financial uncertainty, they had security.

As he hugged me, the man said, "I can't thank you enough. We almost welcome these hard times, because we have such tremendous opportunities to make our contribution dollars count where ministries have significant needs. And for those of us with cash reserves, the opportunities in my business are beyond comprehension."

My firm recently hired an outstanding young man who wanted to change careers. He had earned an excellent income in real estate syndication during the 1980s. A few years ago, he read my first book, *Master Your Money*, and determined that he would get out of debt while he was making a lot of money. So he paid off all his debt, including his home mortgage. When the Tax Reform Act of 1986 killed the real estate syndication business for all practical purposes, this young man found himself out of a job and out of an industry.

Fortunately, he had the cash reserves to withstand the loss, and when he asked to come work for our organization, he was able to start at an entry level at 25 percent of his former salary. He has done well with us, his income has increased steadily, and he will again be financially successful. And while his wife went back to work during his time of unemployment so their children could stay in private school, she is now able to be a homemaker once more.

> *When you look at your financial situation through the eyes of eternity, you put it into the proper perspective.*

I'm not saying that taming your money monster will be easy or that God will provide a miraculous solution. But the truth of Scripture is that God is in control, Jesus will return, and our life here on earth is temporary at best. When you look at your financial situation through the eyes of eternity, you put it into the proper perspective. When you do that and you take the practical steps described in this book, I believe you'll experience hope, motivation, encouragement, and even excitement.

Before you read further in this book, I would challenge you to read Hebrews 11. Develop the perspective of faith. Be on guard against fear, which causes you to lose perspective, make poor decisions, perform at a subpar level, and in the extreme even become paralyzed.

OBJECTIVES

I have five objectives in writing this book:

1. To help you identify how and why you get into debt and thus avoid getting into more debt;
2. To show you how to get out of debt;
3. To teach you how to decide whether to use credit when making any type of purchase or investment decision;
4. To outline a biblical perspective on credit and debt;
5. To be practical and interesting.

DEFINITIONS

To avoid any misunderstandings as we go along, let's define some key terms:

1. *Debt*: an amount owed
2. *Debtor*: one who owes money
3. *Credit*: the right to borrow
4. *Creditor*: the one who gives credit to another
5. *Borrow*: to enter into a contract to rent money for a specified time period, with the rent being called *interest*
6. *Bankruptcy*: the inability, for whatever reason, to repay debt

7. *Surety*: guaranteeing the payment of someone else's debt

Those aren't dictionary definitions in the truest sense of the word, but they're consistent with both dictionary definitions and biblical usage of the terms. Not all the terms are found in the Bible, of course, but they're commonly used today, and in most cases they're implied in Scripture.

To use all the terms at one time, we could say, "A creditor extends credit to someone who, when he exercises that opportunity by borrowing money, becomes a debtor. If he finds himself unable to repay the money rented, he's bankrupt. To be able to borrow, or to avoid bankruptcy, the debtor may ask someone to go surety for him." It's critical to understand that any time you borrow money, you're renting it just the same as you would rent an apartment, a car, or a house.

It's tough to live wisely in a culture that encourages you to mortgage your future and feed the money monster. It's almost impossible to avoid the use of borrowing when there's so much confusion, conflict, and lack of good training on how to properly use credit from both a secular and a biblical perspective.

Additionally, we tend to make poor financial decisions in the vain hope that they'll meet our real needs. We'll look next at some of those powerful motivators.

CHAPTER TWO

The Road to Debt

According to an article in *Money* magazine, "Michael and Cynthia Proctor never asked for their first credit cards. An offer for four of them showed up in their Huntsville, Texas, mailbox in 1982. At the time, Michael and Cynthia, both now 35, together made $28,850 from his job with the Texas Department of Corrections and from her job with the Huntsville National Bank. Michael was also studying nights for his master's degree in criminology. But for all this schooling, the Proctors had never learned to control debt.

"'We used credit cards for whatever caught our fancy,' recalls Cynthia. The Proctors were especially nonchalant about drawing cash advances. Still they easily made the minimum payments, and when they reached the limit on one card, they just got another.

"By 1985 they owed over $32,000 on 63 credit cards. Most payments were at least six weeks behind. Dunning letters arrived daily.

Stress was tearing the family apart."

Larry Burkett, an expert on financial matters, contends that "credit is never the problem; the misuse of credit is." The Proctors' plight illustrates how the misuse of credit can put a family not only under a lot of stress, but even into bondage. But like Burkett, I'm concerned that trouble with debt is *always and only* a symptom of something else. Thus, if you're going to remedy a debt problem, it's essential to understand how and why you got into debt in the first place. There are four common causes of problem debt. They're somewhat overlapping, and they're shared by all kinds of people, be they Christian, non-Christian, black, white, poor, wealthy, or whatever. In other words, you may see yourself in more than one category. The causes are

1. a lack of discipline;
2. a lack of contentment;
3. a search for security;
4. a search for significance.

LACK OF DISCIPLINE

Based on my professional experience, I've concluded that most people who find themselves squeezed by consumer debt are there because of a lack of self-discipline.

To illustrate the consequences, assume the following: A hypothetical husband and wife have a first-year salary of $20,000 that increases

Chart 2.1 ■ DEBT GROWTH					
Yr.	Income	Expense	Difference	Total Debt	Total Payment	Payment as % of Income
1	$20,000	$21,000	($1,000)	$1,000	$100	0.50%
2	21,000	22,000	($1,000)	2,000	200	0.95
3	22,000	23,000	($1,000)	3,000	300	1.36
4	23,000	24,000	($1,000)	4,000	400	1.74
5	24,000	25,000	($1,000)	5,000	500	2.08
6	25,000	26,000	($1,000)	6,000	600	2.40
7	26,000	27,000	($1,000)	7,000	700	2.69
8	27,000	28,000	($1,000)	8,000	800	2.96
9	28,000	29,000	($1,000)	9,000	900	3.21
10	29,000	30,000	($1,000)	10,000	1,000	3.45
11	30,000	31,000	($1,000)	11,000	1,100	3.67
12	31,000	32,000	($1,000)	12,000	1,200	3.87
13	32,000	33,000	($1,000)	13,000	1,300	4.06
14	33,000	34,000	($1,000)	14,000	1,400	4.24
15	34,000	35,000	($1,000)	15,000	1,500	4.41
16	35,000	36,000	($1,000)	16,000	1,600	4.57
17	36,000	37,000	($1,000)	17,000	1,700	4.72
18	37,000	38,000	($1,000)	18,000	1,800	4.86
19	38,000	39,000	($1,000)	19,000	1,900	5.00
20	39,000	40,000	($1,000)	20,000	2,000	5.13

Chart 2.2 ■ DEBT REPAYMENT					
Yr.	Income	Expense	Difference	Total Debt	Total Payment	Payment as % of Income
21	$40,000	$36,200	$3,800	$18,000	$3,800	9.50%
22	41,000	37,400	3,600	16,000	3,600	8.78
23	42,000	38,600	3,400	14,000	3,400	8.10
24	43,000	39,800	3,200	12,000	3,200	7.44
25	44,000	41,000	3,000	10,000	3,000	6.82
26	45,000	42,200	2,800	8,000	2,800	6.22
27	46,000	43,400	2,600	6,000	2,600	5.65
28	47,000	44,600	2,400	4,000	2,400	5.11
29	48,000	45,800	2,200	2,000	2,200	4.58
30	49,000	47,000	2,000	0	2,000	4.08

by $1,000 per year. They overspend their income by $1,000 per year, and they pay only the interest on their growing debt each year. The interest rate they pay is 10 percent. Chart 2.1 shows what happens to them over a period of time.

First, what began as a small problem, $100 per year for debt repayments on an income of $20,000, grows over time to $2,000 per year committed to debt repayment. The $2,000 represents 5.13 percent of their total income that is precommitted and can't be used for any other purpose.

Second, because it's taken 20 years to reach

this point, they may have been unaware of their compounding debt problem. Without understanding why, they've probably been experiencing increasing financial frustration as debt repayment takes an ever-increasing percentage of their income.

Third, after 20 years of marriage, this man and woman have one or more children at or near college age. But just as they're approaching the highest financial-need years, they have a decreasing amount of money available to meet those needs. It's easy to see why their lack of self-discipline over a long period might now cause frustration, confusion, conflict, anger, and even rebellion against God. A small problem has grown into a huge headache.

If these people now decide they want to begin repaying their debt over ten years, or $2,000 per year plus interest, they will experience in years 21 to 30 what chart 2.2 outlines. To make that payment in year 21, their total expenses must go down by $3,800 from the previous year, almost 10 percent, even though they received a $1,000 raise. Debt repayment as a percentage of their total income almost doubles. Note further that it's four years before they reach the same level of spending they had prior to choosing to get out of debt. In other words, the choice to start repaying debt means stepping back in their spending to the level at which they had been four years previously. It's no wonder many people throw in the towel at this point and say, "It's not worth the cost to get out of debt!"

The graph following chart 2.2 pictures this couple over 30 years and confirms that a lack of discipline over a long period results in much less money being available when it's most needed.

As bad as this couple's situation looks, it's actually unusual to see people who have a self-discipline problem overspending by only $1,000 per year. That's a minimal level of over-

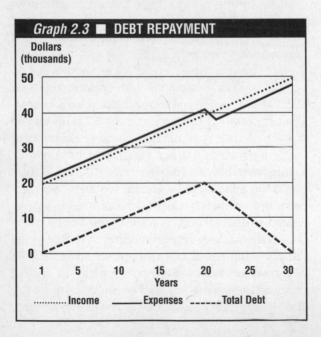

Graph 2.3 ■ DEBT REPAYMENT

Dollars (thousands)

.... Income _____ Expenses ─ ─ ─ ─ Total Debt

spending. For example, the Proctors, described at the beginning of this chapter, went from zero debt to $32,000 of debt within just three years. So our hypothetical case probably understates the real problem. My experience is that most people who lack discipline don't even realize they're overspending, because the one thing that will cure the problem—a budget—is anathema to them.

My hypothetical case also understates the problem in that most consumer debt costs a lot more than 10 percent interest—it's more likely to be 18 or even 21 percent. The example ignores the consequences of taxes and tithe, too. If the couple receive a $1,000 raise per year and pay in taxes and tithe a total of 30 percent, they have only $700 per year in additional spendable income. When receiving a raise, however, most people assume they have the full amount to spend. If they therefore increase their spending by $1,000 per year, they're going into an even deeper hole than what's illustrated.

Being self-disciplined means making the right decisions consistently. Some people are just naturally more self-disciplined than others because of their personalities, and some have learned self-discipline over time. Self-control is also a fruit of the Spirit (see Gal. 5:22-23). Because of what self-discipline is, how it's learned, and how it's applied on a daily basis, there are many ways to acquire it. This book may aid you in the process, but the ultimate solution is up to you.

LACK OF CONTENTMENT

A lack of discipline may be caused by a lack of contentment. The problem could be stated this way: If I lived someplace else, had something else, or did something else, I would be content. But contentment is really a choice. As it says in Hebrews 13:5, "Keep your lives free from the love of money and be content with what you have, because God has said, 'Never will I leave you; never will I forsake you'" (NIV).

Contentment is really a choice.

Many things cause discontent. Reading and believing ads is a common cause. Another is browsing in shopping malls, which can raise your level of discontent to the point that it becomes almost impossible not to yield to the temptation to buy. It's the same as putting a drink in front of an alcoholic. It's no coincidence that the level of personal debt and the amount of time people spend in front of television and in shopping malls have both increased dramatically in the last 30 years.

Many years ago, after I had become a Christian, left a successful business, and moved to Atlanta to enter full-time ministry work, I found myself in a position of great discontent. When we left our hometown, we also left a big house and a fairly large income to move into a much smaller home at a much lower salary. I assumed, however, that being in "God's work," I would be content. I was wrong. Instead, I was very unhappy, especially with the home we had.

The primary problem was that as our children got older and bigger, the house got smaller. Thus, we wanted to move to a larger one. I had just paid off the mortgage on our home, though, so it didn't make economic sense to move. Nonetheless, that fact did not take away the discontent.

For two years we had a "house for sale" sign in our lawn. Then one day, while I was mowing the yard and passing that sign every couple of minutes, I asked God why we had had virtually no lookers at our house in two years. Suddenly this Scripture came to mind: "Not that I speak in regard to need, for I have learned in whatever state I am, to be content: I know how to be abased, and I know how to abound. Everywhere and in all things I have learned both to be full and to be hungry, both to abound and to suffer need. I can do all things through Christ who strengthens me" (Phil. 4:11-13). Paul said he had *learned* to be content.

I realized then that contentment was a choice I had to make. I pulled the sign out of the yard and put it in the garage, choosing to be content where we were unless God moved us. He did move us several years later, and I can truthfully say that during the wait, I no longer had any discontent with where we lived. That's the essence of contentment—choosing to believe God is in control and has us, in all our circumstances, exactly where we should be to learn what He wants us to learn.

SEARCH FOR SECURITY

Deuteronomy 31:8 declares, "The LORD himself goes before you and will be with you; he will never leave you nor forsake you" (NIV). That's God speaking, and if that promise doesn't give us security, nothing will. The problem is that most of us have an earthly perspective and equate security with possessions, a home, food, clothing, a job, a career, a car, children—something other than an eternal relationship with God.

One of the financial planners in my office has been working with a couple in the Northeast who inherited a large sum of money a few years ago. He told me the wife had spent almost the entire inheritance buying and then decorating a new home. She's searching desperately, he explained, for the security of a home that she never experienced as a child. Having almost depleted their small fortune, the couple seemed to think borrowing was the only way they could maintain their life-style.

Men often evidence a search for security by their desire to participate in get-rich-quick schemes. I've seen many Christians compromise their standards and good judgment to try to achieve quickly the "financial independence" they think will make them secure. But being able to earn even hundreds of thousands of dollars a year by exploiting others will never provide ultimate security.

If we can come to grips with the reality that we *are* secure in Christ, however, we'll realize that nothing of a temporal nature will ever meet this very real need. There's no reason to "do" or to "acquire" for the sake of security, because the need has already been met. What I would call the "temporal toys" will never satisfy anyway. Knowing we're secure can also solve the problem of discontent by freeing us to choose to be content.

There's no reason to "do" or to "acquire" for the sake of security, because the need has already been met.

One of my daughters has a poster on her wall that says: "Don't take life too seriously. It is only a temporary situation." That may not be right out of the Bible, but it's good doctrine.

SEARCH FOR SIGNIFICANCE

The drive for significance is another reason people make foolish financial decisions. In my observation, this is more of a male problem than a female problem. As a man myself, I can readily identify with the drive for significance. It's usually equated with position, possessions, power, and success rather than with God's definition.

Many times men, especially, attempt to achieve significance through investments, businesses, possessions, and sexual conquests. They also try to meet this need through heavy borrowing, which threatens the security of their wives. As has been said, "The only difference between men and boys is the price of their toys."

I spoke to a group of clients recently, and afterward a former client who had been invited to the dinner approached me. He asked if I knew anyone who could lend him some money, because he was on the verge of bankruptcy. This was quite a turnaround for him, since he had retired financially secure from a large corporation.

Following retirement, he had started a new business both to occupy his time and to give him an ongoing sense of worth. The business had done well, which encouraged him to speculate in undeveloped land and other real estate investments using large amounts of borrowed money. Then the economy in his area turned down, and his real estate deals soured. His drive for significance through investments had destroyed his previously secure financial position.

Both security and significance are legitimate needs, but they've already been met by God if we're rightly related to Him. We should heed the words of Matthew 6:25-33:

> Therefore I say to you, do not worry about your life, what you will eat or what you will drink; nor about your body, what you will put on. Is not life more than food and the body more than clothing? Look at the birds of the air, for they neither sow nor reap nor gather into barns; yet your heavenly Father feeds them. Are you not of more value than they? Which of you by worrying can add one cubit to his stature? So why do you worry about clothing? Consider the lilies of the field, how they grow: they neither toil nor spin; and yet I say to you that even Solomon in all his glory was not arrayed like one of these. Now if God so clothes the grass of the field, which today is, and tomorrow is thrown into the oven, will He not much more clothe you, O you of little faith? Therefore do not worry, saying, "What shall we eat?" or "What shall we drink?" or "What shall we wear?" For

after all these things the Gentiles seek.
For your heavenly Father knows that
you need all these things. But seek first
the kingdom of God and His righteous-
ness, and all these things shall be added
to you.

When we attempt to meet our needs in our
own ways, we're working against what God has
promised to do for us.

The Bible not only gives us direction in how
to avoid debt problems, but it also points out
directly the root causes of our difficulties. The
problems of lack of discipline, of contentment,
of security, and of significance are timeless. They
just happen to work themselves out in our culture through getting into debt because of the
ease of borrowing.

CHAPTER THREE

Advertising Illusions

I like to save some of the most outrageous ads I receive in the mail giving me an opportunity to establish more credit or to buy something using credit. One I received from a major credit card company said, "So far ahead in value, it actually pays to use it." All I had to do to receive an extra $2,400 of borrowing power was to complete a brief application and send it in the preaddressed, stamped envelope. According to the ad, I would be making a wise financial decision in so doing. And it sure seems logical to use anything that "pays me."

Why do we believe ads like that? How often have you read an ad or watched a television commercial and known instinctively that what it was promising was misleading at best and possibly even untruthful? Yet *knowing* the ad is an illusion, we choose to deceive ourselves and believe it could be true. The underlying motivation is the desire to meet a need for either security or significance. So we respond by borrowing money, putting ourselves in bondage to debt.

In this chapter I want to point out some of the obvious advertising illusions. Second, I want to look at how we deceive ourselves into believing them. Last, I'll outline our real needs and explain how they will never be met through a product, service, or possession.

ADVERTISING ILLUSIONS

One morning I saw a TV commercial in which a man made a statement that left me incredulous. "You can buy wealth, prosperity, financial freedom, and peace for the rest of your life," he said. I couldn't believe I had heard correctly. Later, however, I saw the ad again and wrote it down to make sure I didn't misquote. All you had to do to achieve those benefits was to send $297. You would then receive a set of tapes telling you how to make bundles of money. Better yet, you could call the 800 number shown on the screen and charge the $297 to your VISA or MasterCard, and they would send the tapes immediately.

As I continued to watch TV that morning, the next commercial said, "Happiness is just a phone call away."

Advertising has great value in making potential consumers aware of opportunities and products. It has done much to promote our consumer-based economy, and I don't mean to question the validity of the industry. However, we need to take a look at the advertising illusions, such as the two above, that promote making foolish financial decisions leading ultimately to the bondage of debt. Most of these deceptions are so obvious they don't require explanation. Yet many of us fall prey to them because we forget their promises aren't true. This list isn't meant to be all-inclusive; rather, it's representative of what we see and hear daily.

"You Can't Live Without It"

I often say facetiously that I can resist anything but temptation. The advertising message that you can't live without some product is similar. I find myself not even desiring things until I see them in an ad. Then I begin to feel I can't live without them, which is exactly what the advertisers want. (I'm particularly susceptible to ads for cars, exotic vacations, and electronic toys like VCRs.) If I could avoid the ads, I probably wouldn't even be tempted. But once my desires have been aroused, it's difficult to resist the temptation to buy. Different products will tempt different people, of course, but the underlying message is the same for all: "You can't live without it."

"Why Should You Deny Yourself?"

This type of ad implies that you really do owe it to yourself and there's no good reason not to "get what you deserve." The appeal is to the innate selfish desires we all have. Because it makes so much sense to those natural desires, it may be the most beguiling illusion. Why *should* you deny yourself? The answer is that you never should unless you're governed by the Spirit of God, who provides the power to live a self-disciplined and self-controlled life.

> ### *Remember that advertising is geared to serve the advertisers, not you.*

"Enjoy Now, Pay Later"
This pitch is closely related to the previous one in that it implies you owe it to yourself to enjoy something *now*. And because you can pay later, there's supposedly no real cost to buying when you don't have the cash. This deception plays on the desire for instant gratification. And while you may enjoy the product now, that enjoyment will rarely offset the real cost of ending up in a painful bondage to debt.

"There's Little or No Cost Involved"
There is no such thing as buying something at no cost. You might inherit something or experience a windfall, but if you're going to buy anything, you're going to pay. This type of ad is so

obvious that we tend to chuckle at it, but the fact is that the pitch works. The company sending the ad described at the beginning of this chapter implied there was little or no cost—there was actually "value"—in using its credit card. The truth, however, is that using its card will cost 21 percent per year in interest.

"This Product or Service Will Meet Your Real Needs"

All of us try to meet our real and perceived needs by the ways we spend our money and time. Advertisers know we need things like security, comfort, and companionship, and they exploit our needs by implying that a particular product or service will meet them.

A staff member showed me an ad that said, "Sometimes the greatest reward of personal recognition . . . is instant gratification." The pitch was for an executive membership in a hotel's credit card program, and it made an incredible play on a person's need for significance, promising all kinds of prestige to those who held such a card.

A product may in fact cause us to feel good about ourselves or our circumstances for a while, but no product or service will ever meet the real needs of life. No "thing" can be totally satisfying.

You can undoubtedly think of other advertising illusions. And there are no doubt ones to which *you* are particularly susceptible. The point is not to identify all of them but to remind you that advertising is geared to serve the advertisers, not you. Therefore, advertising uses whatever means are available to get you to make a decision, even though it may not be in your best interest.

PERSONAL RESPONSIBILITY

When we choose to believe that something or someone will meet our needs, we make foolish financial decisions leading to debt. This is so important that I want to repeat it: We usually go into debt because we believe that buying a product or service will meet our real needs. This fact points to two others:

1. Behavior follows belief.
2. No one but you is responsible for your debt situation.

Sure, advertisers use whatever means they can to influence you, but they're not responsible for your choices. You and you alone are responsible for your decisions, just as I'm solely responsible for mine.

Our need to accept responsibility is similar to what alcoholics experience. Not until they take personal responsibility for their decision to drink can they hope to get sober. And only when you and I take personal responsibility for going into debt can we hope to start working our way out of it.

REAL NEEDS

Many counselors, Christian teachers, and psychologists have written about the real needs, other than the basic physical needs, that must be met for people to have true contentment. All of these can be summarized in the two categories identified in the last chapter: the need for security and the need for significance.

When we believe we're secure and significant, nothing needs to be added to our lives to increase our contentment. Yet most of our activities, financial and nonfinancial, revolve around trying to satisfy those needs. No amount of possessions or activities, however, will ultimately meet those needs.

> *You and you alone are responsible for your decisions, just as I'm solely responsible for mine.*

Consider the late Howard Hughes. When he died, he was one of the world's wealthiest individuals, but he lived his final years a total recluse, paranoid about his personal safety. Many stories have been written about how he tried to protect himself from illness and from individuals who might harm him. He was driven by the need for security, yet no amount of wealth could buy him the security for which he longed. He died an insecure, lonely man.

Not long ago, I visited one of the wealthiest individuals in the world today. (I'll call him Ken.) The week following my visit, he was scheduled to have lunch with another man who reportedly is *the* world's wealthiest person. While discussing the upcoming luncheon, Ken said he wasn't really looking forward to the meeting, as people like the man he was having lunch with intimidated him. I thought to myself when Ken said that, *How much wealth does it take for someone to feel significant?*

The answer, of course, is that wealth can't give a person true significance any more than it can give real security. The same can be said of companions, possessions, prestige, or anything else. Ultimately we find our significance in our relationship with Christ. He is the Son of God, and the Bible tells me I am called His brother by adoption into God's family, and also His joint heir. That, and that alone, is true significance. Debt-based accumulation pales in comparison to all I am and have in the person of Jesus Christ.

I'm reminded of the Pharisees in the New Testament. Through their position as leaders and their strict observance of the Mosaic law, they deluded themselves into thinking they were both secure and significant. Nothing could have been further from the truth.

My desire is that you not delude yourself

into believing what the advertising industry says about security and significance. I don't want you to make foolish financial decisions in an attempt to acquire something that cannot be acquired—only received. That's a personal relationship with the Lord Jesus Christ. He said in John 10:10, "I have come that they may have life, and that they may have it more abundantly." He explained in John 3:16, "For God so loved the world that He gave His only begotten Son, that whoever believes in Him should not perish but have everlasting life."

Please take the time now to consider whether you have entered into a personal relationship with God through Jesus Christ. If you haven't done so, I invite you to read Appendix A and respond accordingly.

Then accept responsibility for your debt situation. Don't blame the advertisers; don't blame your spouse; don't blame your parents; and don't blame your children. You alone are responsible. In the past you've made financial decisions believing erroneously that they would meet a real need.

A particularly strong word to us husbands is that our wives generally have a greater need for security than for significance. We, on the other hand, usually have a greater need for significance—that's the way God has wired us. Thus, we need to take care to provide the sense of security our wives need and deserve.

One of the ways we undermine their sense of security is by taking on more debt than we should or than they're comfortable with. Part of our responsibility as godly men is to be sensitive to our wives' needs and not take actions we know will make them feel threatened.

Wives also need to be challenged. A woman can actually undermine her family's financial security—as important as that is to her—by overspending to meet her need for significance. Her legitimate desire to express herself through her home and her decorating ability, if funded by debt, can cause serious strains. Besides, a home and furnishings won't meet her real needs any more than cars or investments will meet a man's.

Accepting personal responsibility for past decisions isn't easy, but it's the first step in getting out of a debt problem. It's also the way to avoid getting into debt trouble in the first place. In later chapters, we'll deal with the question of when borrowing seems to make sense and how it can be used wisely. But for now, I challenge you to sign the statement below in front of a witness:

I understand that I, and I alone, am responsible for choosing to use debt in an attempt to meet my real needs.

Signature _____ Date _____

Witness _____ Date _____

CHAPTER FOUR

Financial Deceptions

We met Tom and Sue briefly in chapter 1. Now let's look at their story in more detail. They married young, while Tom was still in college. Sue worked to pay the household expenses, and he worked summer jobs. That money, with a little help from his parents, put him through school at a state university. Their budget was tight, but they lived within their means.

Once Tom graduated and they were both working (he as a salesman, she as a payroll clerk), they started buying all the things they had done without before: a TV, stereo, new car, and so on. Like many young couples, they spent all they made and more. Credit was easy to get. As long as they could make the payments, they figured they were doing fine. They gave no thought to saving for the future, so they had virtually nothing in savings.

Tom and Sue's life-style was never lavish, but they overspent their income by about $500 per year, year after year. Vacations, appliance replacements, and car repairs always went on credit cards; they never saved ahead for such things.

After 15 years of marriage, they find themselves about $7,000 in debt, mostly in the 18 percent interest range, and they're beginning to wonder if they will ever get out from under it. They're paying about $240 a month total on five different accounts, but the balances seem to be creeping down at best. Their yearly gross income is $35,000.

History proves that there are economic cycles.

Besides their debt, Tom and Sue's biggest current financial concern is their two cars. Both are more than ten years old and in need of major repairs. Tom and Sue wonder if it's worthwhile to make the repairs, because even if they're made, the cars will still be undependable. They also don't have the $1,200 needed to make the repairs, but neither do they have the money to replace the cars. Until now, their response would have been to put the repairs on their credit cards once again and hope that before too long they could replace the cars.

Sally, one of their daughters (they have two), needs braces, too (about $1,800). The orthodontist would let Tom and Sue pay them off at $100 a month.

Their monthly budget is tight; their single largest expense is a house payment of $875. They still don't save anything and don't see how they can.

Their question is, "How do we get out of debt and stay out?" My advice is simple but not simplistic.

More deception (most of it unintended) is perpetrated by accountants, bankers, business schools, and businessmen regarding the use of debt than most of us realize. We tend to respect these professional people. Yet they only pass on what they've been taught, and in many cases they've been taught half-truths. And people like Tom and Sue have bought into them.

Being a CPA, former banker, alumnus of a graduate business school, and businessman myself, I remember what I was taught and have in turn taught others in times past. And there are four major financial deceptions conveyed implicitly or explicitly by my peer group. They are as follows:

1. Borrowed money is always paid back with cheaper dollars in the future.
2. The tax deductibility of interest makes using debt a wise thing to do.
3. Inflation is inevitable; therefore, it is always wise to buy now at a lower cost than in the future at a higher price.

4. Leverage (debt) is magic.

Perhaps I'm too critical to call these deceptions, because they may or may not be true depending on certain assumptions. But the assumptions underlying the four statements are not adequately explained. So to better understand the whole issue of using debt wisely (if, in fact, you should use it at all), you must recognize these deceptions and be able to evaluate them relative to your own circumstances.

DECEPTION 1: PAYING BACK WITH CHEAPER DOLLARS

In the 1970s and early 1980s, inflation was at double-digit levels and was projected by almost everyone to be ever increasing. The "wisdom" then was that you would always be able to pay back borrowed money with dollars that were worth less in the future, because inflation eats away at the purchasing power of money. This wisdom was true as long as two basic assumptions were met. The first was that you were able to borrow at a fixed interest rate so your rate did not increase with inflation. The second was that inflation would continue.

The example used most frequently to sell this deception was the purchase of a home using a fixed-rate, long-term mortgage. This does in fact make sense in a time of inflation, because the dollars used to pay back the principal amount borrowed are worth less and less. In addition, when the interest rate is fixed for the life of the loan, you can't be hurt by the increasing interest rates that go hand in hand with inflation. That approach continues to make sense if the two assumptions continue to be valid.

History proves, however, that there are economic cycles. They may not be geographically universal, but they do occur. For example, if you bought a home in the Southwest in the early 1980s, you would have paid a premium price. But when oil prices fell and the economy turned south in the Southwest, the assumption of continuing inflation proved to be wrong.

Other illustrations abound. No one thought farmland would ever decrease in value. Midwest farms in the early 1980s were selling as fast as they came on the market at prices that eventually reached $4,000 per acre. By the late 1980s, however, that same premium farmland could be purchased for $1,200 to $1,500 per acre.

In the early 1970s, real estate of all forms in the Rustbelt of the Northeast fell dramatically in value as businesses moved to the Sunbelt (where property values increased). But in the mid and late 1980s, the economies in the Northeast and Midwest had recovered sufficiently to be almost classified "boom economies."

The point is that even if inflation were a valid assumption overall, it may not be valid for the region in which you live. When industries leave an area, inflation changes. There aren't as many people demanding the same goods and services, so prices tend to fall. Thus, what is true today regarding inflation may not be true tomorrow.

Lenders push as much of the risk as possible to the borrower.

The idea of gaining an economic advantage by borrowing at fixed interest rates so your rate doesn't go up with inflation assumes that lenders are basically stupid and will continue to lend money at low, fixed rates for long terms even during times of inflation. That's not the case. In periods of inflation, interest rates rise, and lenders promote adjustable-rate mortgages. They also know that the average home loan will mature (be paid off) within eight years as borrowers sell or refinance. Then the money from the payoff of that mortgage can be reloaned on the same house at a higher interest rate. Additionally, every time they make loans, lenders can charge points and fees that increase their income. Thus, they don't make bad decisions even when they're willing to make fixed-rate loans. They push as much of the risk to the borrower as they possibly can. And in times of inflation, they charge premium rates.

Whenever you borrow money at a premium interest rate, the fact of paying back with cheaper dollars in the future is mitigated by the high rate. In my 20 years of professional experience, interest rates on credit card and installment debt have never been lower than the inflation rate except for very short periods. So while you may repay the loan with cheaper dollars in the future, the premium interest rates charged more than offset the benefit.

DECEPTION 2: THE TAX DEDUCTIBILITY OF INTEREST

This deception says that because interest is tax deductible, it's a good idea to have interest expense in order to reduce income taxes. There's a certain amount of truth to that, but it doesn't present the whole picture. First, not all interest is 100 percent tax deductible. Consumer interest (credit cards, car loans, installment loans) isn't, and even investment interest has limitations. The only 100 percent deductible interest is home mortgage interest, and that has limits, too, when the mortgage goes above a certain amount.

Second, to say that an amount is deductible means only that it's deducted from income before computing the taxes owed. It doesn't mean that taxes are offset dollar for dollar by the amount of interest. For example, if you pay a total of 30 percent in state and federal income taxes, then for every dollar of fully deductible interest you pay, you reduce your taxes by $.30, not $1.00. Thus, the net cost of paying interest is $.70 rather than $1.00, but it's still a net cost, and it's *never* a benefit. To say that interest is tax deductible and therefore a good idea actually means it may offer a *partial* benefit.

To clarify whether you should borrow based on the fact that interest offers a tax deduction, I propose this agreement: If you'll loan me $1,000, I promise to never repay you. That way you can deduct the $1,000 as a bad debt expense and reduce your taxes accordingly. I, on the other hand, will keep the $1,000, report it as income, and pay the taxes. You tell me which of us will be better off. Interest deductions operate the same way.

DECEPTION 3:
IT WILL COST MORE LATER

Again during the 1970s and early 1980s, when inflation rates were relatively high, a common advertising theme was "Buy now, because it will cost more later." In fact, it *would* cost more later. However, that ploy begs the true question, which is not "What will it cost later?" but "Do I really need it?"

The second aspect of this deception is the underlying assumption that everything will continue to go up in price. That's not always the case. Personal computer prices, for example, tend to start high when a new model is introduced and then fall steadily. And almost everything goes on sale periodically.

The way to understand the real question when tempted by this deception is to ask, "So what?" In most cases, the answer to that question is "I may not need it later" or "The future price makes no difference to me, because I have to have it." But making a purchase on the basis of its costing more later is a very short-term perspective and may well be a financial mistake.

DECEPTION 4:
THE MAGIC OF LEVERAGE

In graduate school, I was taught the value of OPM—the use of other people's money. The idea is that if you use debt to purchase something, you get a far greater return on your portion of the investment than you would if you paid all cash for it.

The classic example has again been the purchase of a home. If you were to purchase an $80,000 home and put 10 percent down, you would have a net investment of your own money of $8,000. If that home then appreciated 10 percent in one year (meaning you could sell the house for $88,000), you would have a 100 percent return on the money you invested (an $8,000 gain on an $8,000 investment). If, on the other hand, you paid cash for the home, you would have achieved only a 10 percent return (an $8,000 gain on an $80,000 investment). The difference between a 100 percent return and a 10 percent return is the magic of leverage.

During inflationary times, "sophisticated" people expanded the concept to say that it was always unwise to use your own money and always wise to borrow as much as you possibly could for whatever purpose. Those who didn't understand the risks and assumptions bought into the idea.

This concept *will* work as illustrated *if* the underlying assumptions hold true. The basic assumption is that there *will* be appreciation rather than depreciation on whatever is purchased—an idea I've already shown to be false.

The second assumption is that if you borrow money instead of paying cash, you have an alternative use for the money that will yield a return greater than your cost of money. Borrowing to buy a car at 12 percent interest, for instance, assumes that you can earn more than 12 percent by investing your money. But the only way you can earn that kind of return is to put your money at substantial risk.

Many people have gone bankrupt trying to take advantage of leverage. They didn't understand the real assumptions they were making. Even huge lending institutions all over this country have gone bankrupt because they lacked this understanding.

Leverage can work for you, but it's like rid-ing an alligator: It's a lot easier to get on than it is to get off safely.

The best way to conclude this chapter is to advise you that if a deal sounds too good to be true, it probably is. Second, be very careful when accepting counsel from anyone, including supposedly knowledgeable business and professional people. Truly successful people become well off not by using complex techniques or even by reducing their taxes to nothing. Instead, they become successful the old-fashioned way: They earn it. As I said in my first book (*Master Your Money*), the key to financial success is to *spend less than you earn and do it for a long time*. There are *no* shortcuts to taming the money monster.

CHAPTER FIVE

A Biblical Perspective

When I was practicing as a CPA in Indiana, my firm did a lot of bank auditing and consulting work. As a result, I got to know many small-town bankers. One I met in the early 1970s was a young man who had worked in all the departments and through the years assumed increasing responsibilities. Recently his bank was sold to a much larger bank.

The new bank, a good one, wants to build the retail side of its business—that is, consumer lending. Over the next several years, it wants to greatly increase its credit card and installment loan portfolios.

But that raises a serious question for my friend, who's a committed Christian. On the one hand, he's an excellent banker with a chance to become the CEO of his company in the near future. On the other hand, he wonders if encouraging individuals to take on personal debt is consistent with biblical principles. He wrote me a letter recently and asked,

"Can a Christian be a banker?"

Trying to discern if he can be true to his spiritual convictions and still promote a business he has serious questions about, my friend has asked many respected Christians for their counsel. He's discovered to his frustration that there's not much clear understanding of, or consensus on, the biblical teaching about debt. I know how he feels.

As my friend's experience shows, there is considerable misunderstanding of the biblical perspective on borrowing and related issues. Not only is there misunderstanding, but there's also much inconsistency within the Christian world, where the teaching often decries debt. Many Christian organizations, however, use credit cards to operate a part of their ministries. Those that sell materials such as books and tapes often accept credit cards for payment.

Churches spend lots of money employing professional fund-raisers to help them set up programs for the members to fund new structures and building improvements. These encourage the members to take on debt (corporately) and invest in church bonds to fund the improvements. And recently we've seen the advent of "Christian" banks that promote borrowing by individual believers and Christian institutions.

There's also a lack of training by our Christian leaders on this vital topic. I have heard of few sermons on debt, and I see three reasons for the dearth of teaching. First, the pastor himself may not understand debt. Second, he may be subject to the bondage of debt. Third, only a couple of well-known Christian authors have offered a clear, biblical position on debt.

It's also my observation that those who *have* taught in this area are frequently misunderstood. I myself often feel I've been misinterpreted. To approach this topic, then, I will

1. outline what the Bible *does not* say about debt;
2. explain what the Bible *does* say;
3. examine the Bible to see *why* people enter into debt;
4. summarize the biblical perspective on debt.

WHAT THE BIBLE DOES NOT SAY ABOUT DEBT

There are many things the Bible does not say about this subject. The following list is not all-inclusive, but it's a good starting point, because this is where most misunderstandings occur.

It's a Sin to Borrow

The Bible *does not* say it's a sin to borrow money. Before you react to that statement one way or the other, let me assure you that the Bible does give many *warnings* about being in debt. However, it doesn't say you are out of God's will or have violated a commandment when you borrow. You may have violated a biblical principle and therefore must bear the consequences, but there's no indication you need forgiveness for having violated one of God's commandments. That's the difference between an *unwise* decision and a deliberate decision to *disobey* God's orders. And in some cases, like that of Phil and Jenny—the couple whose small business went bankrupt and who ended up owing thousands of dollars to their lawyer (which they had no way of planning for)—debt may simply be unavoidable.

> *There's misunderstanding and much inconsistency within the Christian world.*

Romans 13:8 is the verse generally used to "prove" it's a "sin" to borrow money: "Let no debt remain outstanding, except the continuing debt to love one another, for he who loves his fellowman has fullfilled the law" (NIV). That verse, however, is dealing not with money issues but with relationships. The principle of having a debtor-creditor relationship does change the way we can, and should, respond to both Christians and non-Christians. However, the verse doesn't say you've committed a sin when you borrow money. (On the other hand, Scripture is clear that when you borrow, you may well not be experiencing God's *best* for you. We'll cover this issue in the section on what the Bible *does* say.)

It's Wise to Borrow

A second thing the Bible *does not* say about borrowing money is that it's wise. Leverage is not biblically condoned as "the way" to prosperity. Many Christians have fallen prey to the misuse of leverage. They believe it's the wise way to conduct business and personal affairs. But absolutely nowhere in the Scriptures are we advised or commanded to use debt to accomplish God-given economic goals. On the contrary, there are many warnings against the use of debt.

Early in my practice as a financial planner, I met with a young real estate developer who was getting ready to declare bankruptcy. He had earned a significant income every year, yet he was planning to declare bankruptcy the next week. When I asked how that could be, he made a comment I'll never forget: "Anyone can make money during times of inflation if he's willing to take the risk of high leverage." Unfortunately for him, the economy in his area had become very weak when he was the most highly leveraged, and he was unable to sell the properties he had developed. His cash flow dried up, he couldn't continue making the payments on his properties, and the lenders began calling his loans. Despite a college education and access to the best financial advisers money could buy, his only alternative at that point was to declare bankruptcy. After 15 years of business, he had nothing. The obvious question is, how can such a thing happen to an intelligent businessman with a lot of good financial advisers?

A less-extreme example I encounter daily is the misconception that the only way to financial security is through home ownership (financed principally by a mortgage). The subtle implication, again, is that the use of leverage is a way to prosperity. Therefore, it must be the wise thing to do. Please do not hear me say it's wrong to have a home mortgage. (I will discuss that issue in detail in chap. 12.) However, the Bible does not say that leverage is the way to prosperity for the home owner, the real estate developer, or anyone else.

God Will Bail You Out of Debt

Another thing the Bible *does not* say is that God is obligated to bail us out of debt. Many people I encounter who are heavily indebted have the impression that God has promised to get them out of their problems. The verse quoted most often is Philippians 4:19: "And my God shall supply all your need according to His riches in glory by Christ Jesus." That promise is true, of course, and God *will* meet our needs. But He doesn't promise to overcome the consequences of our unwise behavior.

The most vivid illustration I can think of is this: If you jump off the top of a 25-story building and then claim Philippians 4:19 for deliverance, God is not obligated to rescue you. He doesn't usually interfere with the natural laws He established. He made them for our good, so He allows us to live with the consequences when we violate them.

It's the same way with being in debt. I don't want to appear harsh or cruel, but we must not try to manipulate God into doing something He has not promised to do. He is faithful and certainly will do what is best for each of us. But what He knows to be best and what we believe to be best may not be the same thing. Additionally, He has given us free will and lets us live with the consequences of our choices.

Debt Is an Exercise in Faith

The fourth thing the Bible *does not* say is that the use of debt is an exercise in faith. The underlying assumption here is that because you'll have to pay debt back in the future from resources you don't already possess, you have to trust God to provide them. I most often hear this rationale from pastors who are getting ready to go into a bond program to raise money for a new church building. They tell me they're taking a tremendous step of faith by obligating themselves to pay back the debt. I have never seen a scriptural basis for this belief, however. I personally think it's a direct *contradiction* of Scripture. Rather than being a mark of faith, it's testing God, which we're warned not to do.

My strong conviction, therefore, is that to say we're exercising faith by borrowing money is wrong. It's the same as saying God *needs* to use a lender to meet our needs. It's true He *could* use a lender to meet our needs, but in many cases we put the lender in the place of God and allow him to meet the desires of our heart as opposed to our true needs.

It's a Sin to Loan Money

Just as the Bible doesn't say it's a sin to borrow money, so it doesn't say it's a sin to loan money. Without question, a debtor-creditor agreement changes the relationship between two parties. Anyone who has borrowed money knows the feelings of dread that surround being in debt. It's no fun. Thus, when you loan someone money, you inevitably change your relationship with that person.

Although it's not wrong to loan someone money, I suggest you do two things if you're considering it. First, determine if the borrower has a legitimate need (as opposed to a desire or an opportunity). If there's a legitimate need, such as for shelter, food, or clothing, *give* the money with no thought of repayment. If you can't afford to give it, think seriously before you loan it, because you will have changed the relationship between the two of you. Again, loaning money isn't a sin, but you may miss God's best for your life and the borrower's.

WHAT THE BIBLE DOES SAY ABOUT DEBT

This next section may be the most important part of the book, because it will establish a biblical framework for evaluating borrowing decisions. In addition to financial principles from the Bible, we'll consider many nonfinancial principles that have a bearing on debt.

Paul said in 1 Timothy 5:8, "But if anyone does not provide for his own, and especially for those of his household, he has denied the faith and is worse than an unbeliever." That is both a commandment and a principle that may outweigh any financial consideration when it comes to making a borrowing decision.

The Bible does not say God is obligated to bail us out of debt.

To illustrate: I have recommended in the past that a family with a handicapped child borrow to buy a van in which to transport the child.

That, to me, is a noneconomic decision that overrides the "foolishness" of borrowing to buy a depreciating asset. Some may argue (justifiably) that if the church were doing its job, that family would not need to borrow, because the money would be provided by the church body.

A father may be forced into borrowing on a short-term basis to provide for his family because of illness or some other economic hardship. Perhaps, for example, the father has lost his job.

Or take Betty, the single parent mentioned in chapter 1 who is unable to meet all her obligations. Borrowing to send her children to a Christian school makes no economic sense, but it may make sense from a priority standpoint. She has determined that raising her children in a godly manner is much more important than the financial priority of avoiding debt. I don't think any of us would or could argue with her reasoning.

In each of those cases, the breadwinner is providing for his family as God commanded. But there's a big difference between meeting the family's needs (food, shelter, clothing, medical care) and meeting its desires (vacations, entertainment, houses, cars). The problem is not with borrowing to meet needs, but with borrowing unwisely and contrary to scriptural warnings.

The Bible *does* say three things that have a direct bearing on borrowing decisions:

1. It's wrong not to repay debts.
2. It's foolish to be in a surety situation.
3. Debt may violate two biblical principles that are paramount in our relationship with our Lord.

All Borrowing Must Be Repaid

Psalm 37:21 states, "The wicked borrows and does not repay." The conclusion from this verse is obvious: If you borrow money, you have no alternative but to repay all amounts borrowed. If you don't, by definition you're what the Bible calls "wicked."

An obvious question arises at this point: Is it wrong for a Christian to declare personal bankruptcy? To answer, we need to separate the moral from the ethical (i.e., the biblical from the legal). Our legal system allows individuals and businesses to have some protection from creditors through the various bankruptcy laws. However, I don't believe a Christian can *not* repay the money he has borrowed and still be moral. Failing to repay is to violate the principle in Psalm 37:21.

On the other hand, there *may* be situations in which the legal system can be used for protection until debts can be repaid. But even though the law (ethics) would allow you to pay less than what is owed, or to pay back with no interest accruing while the legal process works itself out, morally you are obligated to repay 100 percent of the money borrowed *according to the interest terms originally agreed upon*. Although it seems impossible to them at this point, just a short time after their bankruptcy, that is Phil and Jenny's sincere desire.

Another Christian businessman who declared bankruptcy is Walt Meloon, the founder of Correct Craft Boats. Through a series of circumstances following World War II, Walt and his brother were forced to declare bankruptcy for their company. Then they were able to reorganize their company under the protection of bankruptcy. And even though they weren't obligated to repay anything to their creditors, they spent the next 25 years searching out and repaying every creditor every penny that was owed. Walt later wrote a book called *Saved from Bankruptcy* that's a testimony to his commitment to follow through on his Christian responsibility.

Surety Is Foolish

In reading the book of Proverbs, specifically 6:1-5 and 11:15, I wouldn't go so far as to call surety (guaranteeing another's loan) a sin, but it is explicitly warned against. As a matter of fact, Scripture advises that if you find yourself in a surety situation, waste no time getting yourself out of it. I suppose we could split theological hairs and argue whether or not surety is a sin. It seems to me, however, that even if it isn't a sin, with such a strong scriptural warning, it makes absolutely no sense to be in a surety agreement.

My counsel about guaranteeing another's loan, therefore, is that if you do it, set aside the money in a separate account, and absolutely expect to have to repay that debt. If you're unwilling to go that far, you certainly should not guarantee the loan, because it's the same thing as entering into the debt yourself. Thus, to not repay is again a violation of Psalm 37:21.

A particularly difficult question regarding surety is whether to guarantee a loan for a relative, especially a child. My counsel is still the same: You should put the money aside and be willing to repay the lender with no thought of repayment by the relative. And remember that going surety for someone changes the relationship just as if you had loaned the money yourself. Thus, you need to decide how much you want that relationship to remain as it is, because guaranteeing a loan will change it forever.

Debt Always Presumes upon the Future
If you borrow money and you believe borrowed money should always be repaid, you are implicitly presuming upon the future unless you have a guaranteed way to repay the loan. If you think you *may* have the ability to repay but in fact you don't because your circumstances change, you will have presumed upon the future.

The scriptural admonition is found in James 4:13-15:

> Now listen, you who say, "Today or tomorrow we will go to this or that city, spend a year there, carry on business and make money." Why, you do not even know what will happen tomorrow. What is your life? You are a mist that appears for a little while and then vanishes. Instead, you ought to say, "If it is the Lord's will, we will live and do this or that." (NIV)

When borrowing, you need to ask yourself what assumptions and presumptions you're making about the future. If you assume, for example, that your health will remain good, that your job will continue to provide income, that the asset borrowed against will continue to go up in value, or that the business you own will continue to generate profit, you may very well find yourself in bondage if these assumptions do not work out. Again, a distinction needs to be made: The Bible does not say it's wrong to borrow money, but it *does* say it's wrong to presume upon the future. Thus, presuming upon the future to borrow money violates not only a caution, but also a command.

A logical question comes to mind at this point: Is there any circumstance under which you can borrow money and not presume upon the future? The answer is yes, and we'll talk about those situations in later chapters. But it's also true that all debt presumes upon the future unless there is a guaranteed way to repay.

Borrowing May Deny God an Opportunity

Without question, God is interested in increasing our faith. Also without question, God will meet every need we have. Therefore, I believe that in many cases, borrowing money denies God the opportunity either to meet our needs or to show Himself faithful, thereby increasing our faith.

It's easy, however, to get confused about the difference between a need and a desire. Desires involve the emotions and are very, very strong. Because they're so strong, they're easily misinterpreted as needs. And when what we have misinterpreted as a need (e.g., the "need" for a vacation) is blocked by a lack of funds, it's not hard to justify borrowing.

Several years ago, my family made a giving commitment that was above and beyond our tithe. When we did our budget planning for the year, however, we realized we would not be able to take our desired vacation in Colorado *and* meet the giving commitment. So we made the decision to cancel our vacation plans and give the money as we had said we would.

Some time after canceling our reservations,

we received a phone call from the owner of the ranch we had planned to visit. He asked if we would consider coming to the ranch *all expenses paid*, including airfare for our family of seven. He explained that they had money set aside to minister to those who they thought would benefit from their facilities and that we were invited to vacation there under that program. We, of course, agreed to go. Subsequently, not only did we receive that invitation, but without making our "needs" known to anyone, we also received *four more* vacation opportunities that year, all expenses paid.

A man named Dan needed to replace an old, worn-out car. But he had read my first book and become convinced that he should not borrow to buy another. (See chap. 11 of this book for the same argument.) He was able to save only $2,000, however, by the time he went looking for a new vehicle. What happened next is a wonderful story of God's provision for someone committed to following biblical principles.

Dan could find nothing in his price range that seemed to be any good. Then the starter on his car went out, just when he was scheduled to go out of town on a business trip. That meant he would have to use the family's second car, stranding his wife. He started his trip on a Thursday.

On Friday, his wife, Jo, found a ride to work with a friend named Connie. During the day, Jo told Connie what was happening, and Connie said she and her husband had an extra car that Jo could drive while her car was being repaired. So Jo got the car and had the transportation she needed while Dan was gone.

Jo liked the car, a 1981 Chevy Monte Carlo with only 34,000 miles on it. After driving it for one day, she decided to give Connie a call and ask if they would consider selling it. Connie replied that the car *was* for sale; they just hadn't gotten around to putting an ad in the paper.

When Dan returned from his trip, Jo told him about the car and asked if he would be interested. He checked it out and concluded that it was in good shape and ought to be safe and reliable. When he asked Connie and her husband how much they wanted for the car, they said they would be happy to get $1,000 for it— half of what Dan had saved. And when Dan looked at the service records, he found they had put nearly that much into the car in the form of new tires, new brakes, and so on in the preceding 16 months.

Dan concluded the story: "You must know by now that I am the proud owner of a 1981 Chevy Monte Carlo. . . . I almost felt guilty about the deal that I had just gotten, but I had to remember that we do have a powerful God and that He had just shown me a miracle. Thank You, God."

That's a great illustration, *but please do not*

hear me say that God will always work in this way.
According to Isaiah 55:8-9, God's ways are not
our ways, and how He chooses to work in our
individual lives is up to Him. He knows what
each of us needs in order to grow our faith. I'm
convinced, however, that if we had not given the
money and had instead taken the vacation, or if
we had given the money and borrowed for the
vacation, God would not have provided as
abundantly as He did.

Sometimes it's difficult to make the hard
decisions, especially when our desires or the
demands of the family are so strong. But choosing to trust God is *always* the best decision.
Hebrews 11:6 is clear in stating, "But without
faith it is impossible to please Him, for he who
comes to God must believe that He is, and that
He is a rewarder of those who diligently seek
Him." Many times the borrowing decision pre-
cludes the opportunity to see how God might
provide, how He might take away the desire, or
even how He may come up with a creative alternative to what we think we need.

The bottom line is this: (1) Don't ever put a
lender in the place of God by depending on the
lender to meet your needs. (2) Don't ever play
God by determining that the only way to meet
your needs is to borrow. That denies God the
opportunity to be who He is. The One who cre-
ated the universe by a spoken word can certainly meet all our financial needs.

From a biblical perspective, we are free to borrow money, but there are consequences we must bear when we do. In other words, God isn't obligated to bail us out of difficulties resulting from foolish decisions.

The nonrepayment of money borrowed is not an option for a Christian. Personal bankruptcy may be warranted in some cases, but never to avoid repayment.

Debt may violate two biblical principles: It almost always presumes upon the future, and it may deny God the opportunity to do what He really wants to do in our lives.

All other principles and commandments of Scripture that aren't specifically related to money may have financial consequences as they are worked out in our lives.

My challenge to you as you look back over this chapter is to review what new thoughts, principles, and truths you were made aware of regarding borrowing money. First, record those thoughts in the space below. Second and most important, write down how what you've learned will affect future borrowing decisions.

Principle	Effect
_____	_____
_____	_____
_____	_____
_____	_____

CHAPTER SIX

The Road Ahead

I once met a retired pastor, 82 years old at the time, who was never paid more than $8,000 per year yet was a millionaire. When I saw him (a visit described in my first book), he asked me if he had enough money to live out the rest of his life. Examining his assets, I found he had over $1,640,000 in cash, stocks, bonds, certificates of deposit, and other liquid investments.

After my first visit with him, I went back and asked for details about how he had been able to do so well on such a small income. One of my first questions was whether he had ever borrowed money. He replied that one time in the 1930s, he had borrowed a little over $300 from a life insurance policy to buy a car. He had paid that loan back within a year. Other than that, he had never borrowed at any time for any reason.

"Why not?" I asked.

"I never felt I could afford to," he said. "I never was sure enough of my income that I felt

I could take on the debt payment. So I never borrowed money."

I also asked what his giving pattern had
been. He indicated he had always given at least
15 percent of his income to the Lord's work. He
had also sent his three sons to college.

When he retired in the early 1960s, he had a
total retirement savings of $10,000. Following
wise counsel, he had invested the money well
and seen it grow substantially. I learned in lis-
tening to him the truth of Proverbs 13:11: "He
who gathers money little by little makes it
grow" (NIV). Had this man and his wife spent
the $10,000, they never would have had it to
invest. Additionally, had they decided to cash in
their investments as soon as they had grown a
little, they could not have continued to increase.

---

*You can spend money any way
you want, but you can only
spend it once.*

In other words, I learned that you can spend
money any way you want, but you can only
spend it once. By not spending it, you have it
available for something else.

Then I asked this pastor what he had
learned in all his years regarding money management. "God is faithful," he responded. I

thought to myself, *That's easy to say when you have $1,640,000,* so I asked him to explain. He answered with a story.

While he was still in seminary, he and his wife had two children, and every Friday the milkman brought the milk those youngsters needed. One particular Friday, however, they had absolutely no money in the house with which to pay the dollar for the milk. As the young seminarian left his apartment that morning, he said to his wife, "We're just going to have to trust God to provide the milk."

Shortly after he left, his wife was standing at the kitchen window when she saw the milkman coming up the back steps. At the same time, there was a knock at the front door. Having to decide which door to open first, she went to the front door, because she knew who was at the back and that she didn't have the money to buy the milk. She opened the front door and found a neighbor standing there.

The neighbor told her that at the Wednesday evening prayer service, she had been placed under great conviction by the Holy Spirit to give a dollar to this couple. She apologized for waiting two days to follow her conviction. The young wife thanked her profusely for her faithfulness to God, took the dollar, walked to the back door, and bought her children's milk!

From that experience, my pastor friend learned that God would always meet their needs, and that anytime he was tempted to meet his needs in his own way in the future, he should just remember that God is faithful. And one way God meets our needs is by helping us learn sound principles of managing the money He's entrusted to us. In this chapter we want to begin considering the specifics regarding debt.

It has been difficult for me, and probably for you, to deal with some of the foundational truths before we begin to answer the *real* question: How do I get out of debt? All of us want to see the final product. But the end result is only as good as the foundation.

To summarize where we are, we have so far concluded the following:

1. Going into debt is a personal decision requiring personal responsibility. The one who made the choice to borrow the money is solely accountable. The first step to getting out of debt, therefore, is taking personal responsibility for going into debt.

2. In most cases, there is no real need to go into debt. Advertising and financial deceptions try to convince us otherwise, but they sound too good to be true because they are.

3. God wants to and will meet each of our real needs. No one and nothing else can.

The next chapter will present the four steps to getting out of debt. Chapter 8 will give you a framework for evaluating the use of credit by identifying the different kinds. It will also provide the criteria for deciding whether or not to use credit.

Chapter 9 will be a transition to the specific decisions regarding debt covered in chapters 10, 11, 12, and 13. The types of debt that will be discussed are

1. credit card debt
2. installment debt
3. home mortgage debt
4. business debt
5. investment debt
6. college debt
7. life insurance debt
8. church debt

We will examine how to evaluate each type of debt in light of the rules developed in chapter 8. We'll also apply the debt decision specifically to the purchase of cars and homes, as these are the two major items most people finance using credit.

Before going on, however, you need to understand something called "the magic of compounding."

THE MAGIC OF COMPOUNDING

Compounding has been called the eighth wonder of the world because it changes a dollar saved for the future into multiples upon multiples of dollars. For example, if you were able to save $1,000 per year, and if you earned 12.5 percent interest each year, at the end of 40 years you wouldn't have just $40,000. The actual amount available to you would be $1 million! This amount excludes the impact of inflation and taxes, but the point remains that *you don't have to save $1 million in order to have $1 million*.

Another illustration is even more dramatic. If you were to make a one-time investment of $10,000, and if you were able to earn 25 percent interest (admittedly an unusually high return) on that $10,000 every year for 40 years, at the end of that time you would have a fund totaling $75,231,638. However, if you were able to earn "only" 24 percent, the fund would be worth "only" $54,559,126. The difference in the amount earned is almost $21,000,000, with 1 percent in interest being the only variable.

Charts 6.1 and 6.2 illustrate the results over time, at various interest rates, of investing either a lump sum of $10,000 or a fixed amount of $1,000 per year.

Graph 6.3 further illustrates how the magic of compounding works and what the variables are. In the beginning, you don't see much growth. But as time goes on, the growth increases significantly. The three variables are the amount, the time period, and the rate of interest. Obviously, the earlier you begin, the more you invest, and the higher your interest, the greater the impact.

Chart 6.1 ■ THE MAGIC OF COMPOUNDING I

Time + Money + Yield
Deposit a Lump Sum of $10,000
Value After a Specified Time Period

Int. Rate	5 years	10 years	15 years	20 years	25 years	30 years	35 years	40 years
2%	$11,040	$12,189	$13,458	$14,859	$16,406	$18,113	$19,998	$22,080
4	12,166	14,802	18,009	21,911	26,658	32,443	39,460	48,010
6	13,382	17,908	23,969	32,071	42,918	57,434	76,860	102,857
8	14,693	21,589	31,721	46,609	68,484	100,626	147,853	217,245
10	16,105	25,937	41,772	67,274	108,347	174,494	281,024	492,592
12	17,623	31,058	54,735	96,462	170,000	299,599	527,996	930,509
14	19,254	37,072	71,379	137,434	264,619	509,501	981,001	1,888,835
16	21,003	44,114	92,655	194,607	408,742	858,498	1,803,140	3,787,211

Chart 6.1 ■ **THE MAGIC OF COMPOUNDING I** *(continued)*

Time + Money + Yield
Deposit a Lump Sum of $10,000
Value After a Specified Time Period

Int. Rate	5 years	10 years	15 years	20 years	25 years	30 years	35 years	40 years
18%	$22,877	$52,338	$119,737	$273,930	$626,686	$1,433,706	$3,279,972	$7,503,783
20	24,883	61,917	154,070	383,375	953,962	2,373,763	5,906,682	14,697,606
22	27,027	73,046	197,422	533,576	1,442,101	3,897,578	10,534,018	28,470,377
24	29,316	85,944	251,956	738,641	2,165,419	6,348,199	18,610,540	54,559,126
25	30,517	93,132	284,217	867,361	2,646,698	8,077,935	24,651,903	75,231,638

Chart 6.2 ■ **THE MAGIC OF COMPOUNDING II**

Time + Money + Yield
Deposit a Lump Sum of $1,000 per Year
Value After a Specified Time Period

Int. Rate	5 years	10 years	15 years	20 years	25 years	30 years	35 years	40 years
5%	$5,525	$12,578	$21,578	$33,065	$47,727	$66,439	$90,320	$120,800
8	5,867	14,487	27,152	45,762	73,106	113,283	172,317	259,056
12	6,353	17,548	37,279	72,052	133,333	241,332	431,663	767,091
16	6,877	21,321	51,660	115,380	249,214	530,312	1,120,713	2,360,757
20	7,442	25,959	72,035	186,688	471,981	1,181,882	2,948,341	7,343,858
24	8,048	31,643	100,815	303,600	898,092	2,640,916	7,750,225	22,728,802

It's essential to understand the magic of compounding because the flip side of investing money is borrowing it. If you borrow money at 12.5 percent, if you pay $1,000 per year in interest to the lender, and if you do that for 40 years, the lender, assuming he can reinvest the money at 12.5 percent, has earned $1 million on your interest payments, even though you have paid him only $40,000 (plus the principal). I call this phenomenon "the opportunity cost of consumption." You can choose to be either a borrower of money, giving someone else the opportunity to

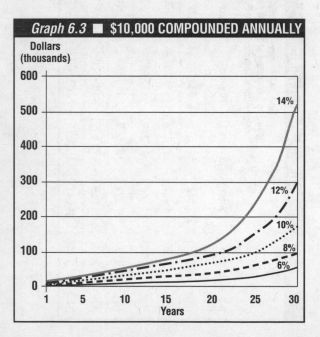

Graph 6.3 ■ $10,000 COMPOUNDED ANNUALLY

earn through the magic of compounding, or a saver, or investor, of money, which is the same thing as being a lender. Then you can see the magic of compounding working *for* you rather than *against* you.

One guaranteed good investment is to pay back all high-cost debt, such as credit card debt that's costing you 12 to 21 percent. That's the same thing as making an investment at 12 to 21 percent. For example, if you have $3,000 in a savings account earning 5 percent and $3,000 of credit card debt costing you 21 percent, the net differential is 16 percent against you. By taking the $3,000 out of your savings account and paying off the 21 percent debt, you're doing the same thing as making a 16 percent investment. If, in future months, you then take the amount that would have been paid to retire the credit card debt and invest it in your savings account, you'll benefit from the magic of compounding.

CHAPTER SEVEN

How to Get Out of Debt

In previous chapters, we have looked at three real-life situations. Tom and Sue, who married young and continued to overspend their income by $500 per year, have decided they now want to get out of debt. We also looked briefly in chapter 1 at a single mother who cannot seem to meet all her priorities without incurring more debt, and also at a couple whose small business failed and saddled them with heavy debts.

In this chapter, we want to see specifically how those families can tame their money monsters. In so doing, I'll explain a few basic, simple steps to getting out of debt so you can see how the process works. The steps are pretty much the same for everyone, so my approach will be to use Tom and Sue's situation as an in-depth case study. What will work for them will also work for Betty, for Phil and Jenny, and for *you*.

You get out of debt little by little over time, and the major requirement is discipline. The most formidable aspect is that *it almost always requires a change in life-style and a reordering of priorities.* That's painful, and the natural human tendency is to resist such change. You may wish there were some easy, painless way to get out of debt. But no such "out" exists. *If you want to be free of a debt problem, you've got to make up your mind, with your family's cooperation, that you'll pay the price now to enjoy financial freedom later.*

The only alternatives to gradual repayment of debt are to sell assets or increase your income. Selling assets may mean selling a car, a boat, a house, an investment, or something else that's providing a level of life-style now. Generating more income may mean putting a spouse to work outside the home (which I don't really recommend as a way to maintain a standard of living, as you'll see below), obtaining a second job for the breadwinner, or asking adolescent children to work part-time. Each of these alternatives requires a change in life-style, as something must be given up—namely, time or possessions.

You get out of debt little by little over time, and the major requirement is discipline.

There are five steps to take in getting out of debt. They're easy to list, hard to do. But there's no other moral way. The five steps are:

1. Determine where you are.
2. Stop going into debt.
3. Develop a repayment plan.
4. Establish accountability.
5. Reward yourself.

STEP 1: DETERMINE WHERE YOU ARE

It's interesting to hear people talk about their debt situation, because most people do not consider either a home mortgage or a car loan as debt. Those two kinds of debt have become such a standard part of our lives that we think of them differently.

The first step to getting out of debt, however, is knowing your *total amount* of debt. In chart 7.1, I have completed a listing of Tom and Sue's total debts. You'll recall that they owe $7,000 on five different credit cards. They also have a home mortgage, but I didn't include that in this debt schedule, as that will be repaid out of their living expenses over the next 15 to 20 years.

A blank schedule is provided at the end of this chapter so you can list all your debts. In addition to your credit card balances, include your installment loan balances, mortgage balances, and any other term note balances you owe. Then you'll have a realistic and honest appraisal of your total debt. In listing the amounts owed, do not include such regular monthly expenses as utilities, school tuition, food, and clothing, as those are normal monthly bills and not debts.

Chart 7.1 ■ DEBT SCHEDULE			
Lender	Amount Owed	Due Date	Payment Schedule
VISA	$3,700	Mo.	75/Mo.
MASTERCARD	$1,900	Mo.	85/Mo.
SEARS	$1,000	Mo.	55/Mo.
DISCOVER	$300	Mo.	15/Mo.
AMOCO	$300	Mo.	10/Mo.

Now that you've listed all amounts owed and you're certain of your commitments regarding debt repayments, you need to do two more things. These are spiritual requirements. First, if anything comes to your mind for which you need to be forgiven by our heavenly Father regarding why and how you got into debt, deal with that. First John 1:9 says, "If we confess our sins, He is faithful and just to forgive us our sins and to cleanse us from all unrighteousness." Confess specifically, asking God for His forgiveness. Then thank Him for the fact that through Jesus Christ you *are* forgiven. Once this has been done, you need never look back and feel guilty, because, being true to His Word, God has forgiven you.

Second, in faith obey 1 Thessalonians 5:18: "Give thanks in all circumstances, for this is God's will for you in Christ Jesus" (NIV). This verse does not mean it's God's will for you to be in debt. But the fact that you're in debt and want to get out of it gives God an opportunity to show Himself faithful as you're obedient to the conviction under which He has brought you. So as an exercise of faith you can give thanks, knowing God is even more eager than you are to have you free from the money monster.

STEP 2: STOP GOING INTO DEBT
This step is extraordinarily difficult to take, I know. It requires a decision that *there will be no additional borrowing for any purpose*. Before you even consider taking on more debt, you should go through the process described in chapter 8 for evaluating the borrowing decision.

If you're an overspender and in debt, however, then even the latter chapters will not be justification for avoiding this step. You absolutely must decide to use debt *no longer*. If that requires destroying your credit cards, my recommendation is simple:

1. Lay your credit cards on a sheet of aluminum foil.
2. Put them in the oven at 450 degrees.

3. In just a few minutes, you'll have a brightly colored mass of plastic.
4. After it cools, hang it in a conspicuous place to remind you of your decision to stop going into debt.

If you're worried about stinking up your kitchen, you can perform "plastic surgery" on your credit cards—that means using scissors to cut up each card into at least eight pieces. And if you're concerned about how you'll get along without credit cards, let me assure you that within just a few months you can have them all back. The credit card companies want you to use their cards. Very shortly they will send you new cards, unsolicited.

This commitment to stop using debt in any form needs to be made both to our Lord and to another person or couple who will hold you accountable (see step 4 for more about this). Hard as it is, Tom and Sue need to make this commitment.

STEP 3: DEVELOP A REPAYMENT PLAN

In addition to knowing your current debt level, you need to learn what your cash flow and your living expenses are per year. On the following pages, charts 7.2 and 7.3 have been completed for Tom and Sue. Again, you'll find blank charts at the end of this chapter for you to complete. Note that Tom and Sue are once more planning to overspend their income by $500 unless they make changes in either their income or one of their spending areas (e.g., giving, taxes, living expenses, or debt repayments).

If you've never before tallied your living expenses in such a manner, go to an office supply store and buy a simple ledger book. It should have at least 31 vertical columns (one for each day of the month) on each two-page spread. List the expense categories down the left-hand side of the spread, and for one month record each day's expenses in each category in the column for that day. At the end of the month, total the expenses in each category on the right-hand side of the spread. For nonmonthly expenses (e.g., car insurance), review your checkbook register and other financial records from the past year.

You should now know where you are from a debt, cash flow, and living expense standpoint. Having also made the commitment to stop going into debt, you can develop a strategy for repaying those debts. There is no one "right way" of repaying your obligations. What follows are several *suggestions*, any one of which (or a combination) might work in your particular situation.

Sell Assets

The first idea for repaying your debts is to determine if there are any assets that can be sold. Even small things that could be sold through a garage sale can help you get out of smaller debts. The sale of bigger items such as cars, investments,

Chart 7.2 ■ LIVING EXPENSE SUMMARY

	Amount Paid Monthly	Other Than Monthly	Total Annual Amount
Housing:			
Mortgage/Rent	875		
Insurance			
Property Taxes			
Electricity	120		
Heating	40		
Water	25		
Sanitation	20		
Telephone	75		
Cleaning			
Repairs/Maintenance			
Supplies			
Other			
Total Housing	1,155		13,860
Food Total	400		4,800
Clothing Total		1,000	1,000
Transportation:			
Insurance		500	
Gas and Oil	150		
Repairs/Maintenance			
Parking			
Other			

Chart 7.2 ■ LIVING EXPENSE SUMMARY *(cont.)*	Amount Paid Monthly	Other Than Monthly	Total Annual Amount
Total Transportation	150	500	2,300
Entertainment/Recreation:			
Eating Out	25		
Baby-sitters			
Magazines/Newspapers		50	
Vacation		500	
Clubs/Activities			
Other			
Total Enter./Rec.	25	550	850
Medical Expenses:			
Insurance			
Doctors	50		
Dentist	25		
Drugs	25		
Other			
Total Medical	100		1,200
Insurance:			
Life		200	
Disability			
Other			
Total Insurance		200	200
Children:			

Chart 7.2 ■ LIVING EXPENSE SUMMARY (cont.)

	Amount Paid Monthly	Other Than Monthly	Total Annual Amount
School Lunches			
Allowances	40		
Tuition			
Lessons	60		
Other			
Total Children	100		1,200
Gifts:			
Christmas		300	
Birthdays		200	
Anniversary		100	
Other			
Total Gifts		600	600
Miscellaneous:			
Toiletries	25		
Husband: misc.	50		
Wife: misc.	50		
Cleaning/Laundry			
Animal Care	25		
Beauty/Barber	15		
Other	100		
Total Miscellaneous	265		3,180
TOTAL EXPENSES	2,195	2,850	29,190

Chart 7.3 ■ CASH FLOW SUMMARY	
Gross Income:	$ 35,000
Less:	
Giving	(1,200)
Taxes (from pay stubs)	(2,230)
Debt Payments (from chart 7.1)	(2,880)
Living Expenses (from chart 7.2)	(29,190)
Cash Flow Margin:	$< 500 >

and perhaps even homes should also be considered. As I said earlier, that may require a change in life-style, *but how badly do you want to be free from the bondage of debt?* Consider starting with small items such as extra clothing, old televisions, games, books—anything you don't need and can sell. (Like most couples, Tom and Sue have a lot of things gathering dust that could go into a garage sale.) When we demonstrate commitment, which is a faith step, our Lord will then show us what the second, third, and fourth steps might be. Selling belongings demonstrates your commitment to change your life-style and tame the money monster.

Use Savings Accounts

Earlier I recommended that you consider using savings accounts or surplus cash balances in checking accounts to pay off debts. Using a low-yielding savings account to pay off high-cost debt is a guaranteed high-yield investment. If you have a savings account and are still carrying credit card or installment debt, consider using those funds to reduce debt.

If you take this approach, replenish your savings accounts as soon as the debt is paid off. Just keep paying the same amount you had been putting toward credit cards and installment debt—only now it goes into your savings.

Double Payments
A third strategy for getting out of debt is to double up on your payments. I recently received a letter from someone who indicated he paid $60 per month on one credit card, thinking he was reducing the debt. In fact, however, he was paying only a few dollars on principal each month and making no real dent in the total owed. But by doubling up on the payments and cutting expenses in another area of the budget, it's possible to pay off debt much more quickly.

In a later chapter, I'll show the benefits of paying home mortgages on a bimonthly schedule, or even making just one extra payment per year. This strategy has a dramatic impact on the number of payments that will be needed to pay off your mortgage.

Keep Payments Constant
A fourth strategy is relatively painless but nonetheless essential: Keep constant the total

amount of payments you're making each month. Concentrate on paying off your smallest debt first. That's the quickest way to be rid of one debt, and it will encourage you to keep going. When that debt is gone, rather than spend the amount freed up by no longer having that payment, apply it to the next-smallest debt (in addition to what you were already paying on that debt). It's like climbing a ladder, beginning at the bottom and working your way to the top.

For example, if you have several credit card and installment payments totaling $500 per month, instead of reducing the amount paid each month as the debts are eliminated, continue to send a total of $500 per month, always increasing the payments to the smallest debt first. As you move up the ladder of debt, the obligations are paid off that much more rapidly.

In the case of Tom and Sue, they are now paying a total of $240 per month on their credit card bills (see chart 7.1). Using this strategy, they might make minimum payments on the larger balances such as those for VISA, MasterCard, and Sears. Then they could take the rest of what they had been paying to those accounts and apply it, first of all, to their Amoco bill, which would probably be paid off in one month. Next, by keeping their payments constant at $240, still maintaining minimum payments to the larger account balances, they could apply all the excess to Discover until it's paid off. Then they could tackle the Sears bill with the same strategy.

Within six months, three of the five credit cards would be paid off. Within 12 months, four of the five would be clear. By the second year, they would be paying off only one card balance; $240 a month to VISA. They may still need 12 to 24 months to eliminate that debt because of the accumulating interest, but it's easier emotionally to have just one credit card to deal with instead of receiving five bills every month.

Reduce Living Expenses

A fifth strategy is to review your living expense summary (chart 7.2) and as a family decide where you can cut expenses. Apply the amount cut to specific debts. You might decide to cut down on your entertainment, clothing, food, or home maintenance budgets—whatever fits your family situation. The fact is that in almost every family budget, as much as 10 to 20 percent could be used to repay debt. Again, it will require a change in life-style, but that cost will be more than offset by the sense of satisfaction in seeing yourself gradually get free of payments.

Reduce Tax Withholdings

A sixth strategy is available if you're now receiving a federal income tax refund each year: Reduce your tax withholdings, and apply the increase in take-home pay to your debt repayment. The IRS does not require you to pay in withholdings (or estimated payments) any more than what you will actually owe. It's a simple matter to decrease your withholding to the amount of the actual projected liability.

Here's how to reduce your withholdings. First, determine your tax liability for the year. Begin by looking at last year's federal income tax return to see how much you paid. Then calculate the effect of any relevant changes this year (a raise; the birth of a child; having an older child become self-supporting; etc.). After you have determined what you're likely to owe in federal taxes, you can have your withholdings decreased to no more than that amount. Simply go to your personnel office and fill out a new W-4 form. Employers are required in some cases to report significant changes in withholding requests to the IRS, but that's no problem if you're using an actual tax projection.

A regular tax refund is a sign of poor stewardship.

The fact is that a regular tax refund is a sign of poor stewardship. You're allowing the government to use your money interest-free, whereas you could be using that same money to pay off high-interest debt. In the cases of Tom and Sue and Betty (the single mom), if either state or federal income taxes are being withheld from their paychecks, it's possible their withholdings could be reduced. This is certainly an area they need to look into as a way of increasing their disposable income.

Do Not Decrease Giving

There may be other strategies you could use, and the ones offered here are only suggestions. The important thing is that you develop your own strategy *and then implement it*. In making your plans for debt reduction, however, there are certain things you absolutely should *not* do.

The first is that you shouldn't decrease your giving to the Lord. This is not the book for a detailed discussion of giving, but the Bible is clear in asserting, "Honor the LORD with your wealth, with the firstfruits of all your crops; then your barns will be filled to overflowing, and your vats will brim over with new wine" (Prov. 3:9-10, NIV). Giving should be the first priority use of money, because it's a recognition of God's ownership of everything. When we acknowledge it's all His, there's nothing more spiritual about giving than paying off debt. However, giving out of the firstfruits maintains the proper perspective on money and money management.

The only time when a reduction in giving to repay debt might be acceptable is if the debt situation is extremely severe, you have prepared a budget that cuts out all surplus uses of money, and the decision to decrease giving is only temporary. Then your decision should be communicated to your pastor, and you should get his agreement on it. In those circumstances, giving may be temporarily decreased. This would be a good idea for Betty, the single mom who will never get out of debt without taking some such action.

Do Not Use Tax Money
Second, do not reduce your tax payments below your projected liability. If you do, you're just borrowing from the government to pay someone else. You aren't really reducing your debt at all. The day of reckoning is merely postponed to the following April 15.

Do Not Use a Debt Consolidation Loan
Third, in most cases you should not take out a debt consolidation loan. The typical reason for such a loan is that it "feels good," but it doesn't solve the basic problem. Many people who go for debt consolidation find they have to come back to it frequently because they have not really solved their spending problems. If you're seeing a debt counselor, however, and the counselor recommends a debt consolidation loan as

your only alternative—and if the counselor will work with you to set up a realistic budget—then it may be appropriate. But it should be a one-time solution.

Do Not Seek a Second Full-time Income

The last recommendation regarding what not to do is the one violated most often by couples. Namely, if the wife is currently a homemaker, she should not get a job to increase the family's income. I have done many studies on working wives, and when you consider the additional expenses of tithing, taxes, child care, transportation, and so on associated with the second job, the economic benefit of a working wife is almost nonexistent. Besides, *most debt problems are spending problems, not income problems*. If a homemaker goes to work to fund a consumptive life-style, the root problems have not been identified and dealt with. Therefore, a second job will provide no long-term satisfaction.

I realize there are exceptions to this general rule: A family may face unexpected medical bills or desire to send their children to a private school for good reasons. In such cases, a working wife may be the means of providing the extra income. Apart from such needs, however, I can see very little *economic* reason for a wife to work outside the home. Given human nature, extra income tends only to raise the level of discontent, increasing the desire for more and more "things" that won't meet real needs.

Another possible exception to the rule is if a wife takes a part-time or temporary job to help pay off debt. This shouldn't be done to fund a higher level of life-style, but on a short-term basis it could be a partial answer to getting out of a squeeze.

Consider Counseling

In severe debt situations, the repayment plan may require professional assistance. There's nothing disgraceful about asking for help. You might be a single mother (like Betty) with several children to support, for example, and increasing your income, selling assets, or decreasing expenses aren't viable alternatives.

The help you need might be found at a local credit counseling agency. Or you might want to contact Christian Financial Concepts, Larry Burkett's counseling ministry. They have trained counselors all over the country. Burkett has also written a book called *How to Get Out of Debt* that you might benefit from reading. See Appendix B for detailed instructions on where to find help.

STEP 4: ESTABLISH ACCOUNTABILITY

An axiom in business says, "Don't expect what you don't inspect." Anyone who has raised children understands the wisdom in this saying. And I've found that even as adults, we benefit from accountability. If you must report to someone you respect on a commitment you've made voluntarily, such as getting out of debt, you're more likely to follow through. If you're unwilling, however, to verbalize to another person your commitment to get out of debt, be it to your spouse or, preferably, another person, the likelihood of your following through is reduced dramatically.

In Tom and Sue's case, they have made their commitment to each other, and they're pretty good at helping one another toe the line. They've also discussed their decision to tame the money monster with their parents and several friends.

The principle of accountability is seen throughout Scripture. When the Lord Jesus sent out His disciples, He sent them two by two. Paul went on his missionary journeys with a partner. Christians are admonished regarding their responsibilities to one another (see, e.g., Gal. 6:9-10). Accountability, logically and legitimately, follows from those admonishments.

Ask someone to hold you accountable, not in a general sense, but specifically to make certain payments on designated dates. Set up a schedule of reporting times. Establish the length of the accountability period. In other words, neither the commitment nor the time is open-ended.

When you ask that person or couple to hold

you accountable, be honest about why you're doing it. You have already asked for and received God's forgiveness, as well as His help, and certainly He isn't critical or condemning. Nor is your accountability partner likely to be. Most people who care about you would be honored to help.

STEP 5: REWARD YOURSELF

Throughout Scripture, we are promised rewards. Many of them are eternal, but others are temporal. I believe our Lord uses rewards because of their motivational value. When we have something positive to look forward to, we're encouraged to maintain the disciplines required to get there. Many people who have trouble losing weight, for example, develop a reward system that motivates them to maintain a diet. In the same manner, it's a good idea to reward yourself as you pay off debt.

When you pay off your first debt, for instance, you might treat yourself to a special lunch. When the second debt is paid off, you could enjoy a nice dinner. When the third debt is paid off, it might be time for a more expensive treat like a weekend away (a pleasure Tom and Sue recently enjoyed). Paying off the fourth or final debt could result in a reward such as clothes or furniture.

Obviously, you don't want to get yourself into more debt through your reward system.

The idea is to find ways to motivate yourself to maintain the disciplines required to get out of debt. They don't have to cost much money—or any at all. You might look forward, for example, to a coupon-book-burning ceremony or to hanging a homemade "Graduation from Debt" certificate on the family-room wall. Whatever the rewards you choose, they need to be personally motivational. The most significant reward will be the financial freedom that comes from getting out of debt.

GETTING STARTED

The steps I've outlined for getting out of debt are simple, but not simplistic. They are all that's required to be relieved of the bondage of debt. The key is to take the first step. Someone once asked, "How do you eat an elephant?" The answer is, "One bite at a time." Getting out of debt is likewise done one step at a time. It may appear to be an impossible task at this point, but I'm convinced that the grace of God is sufficient to meet your every need as you follow these steps.

Since getting started is usually the most difficult part of any task, chart 7.4 is for you to use to begin the process of taming the money monster. The chart below shows Tom and Sue's plan; a blank copy is provided for your use at the end of this chapter. Complete the chart prayerfully and promptly. *Now* is the best time to begin.

Chart 7.4 ■ ACTION PLAN		
Step	**Action**	**Completion Date**
1. Determine where you are.	1. Complete chart 7.2	1. done
	2. Complete chart 7.3	2. done
	3.	3.
	4.	4.
2. Stop going into debt.	1. Destroy credit cards.	1. done
	2. Use cash only.	2.
	3.	3.
	4.	4.
3. Develop repayment plan.	1. Yard sale, pay Amoco.	1.
	2. Sell TV, pay Discover.	2.
	3. $220/mo. to Sears.	3.
	4.	4.
4. Establish accountability.	1. Pray for right person.	1. immediately
	2. Ask him/her.	2.
	3. Set date for meeting.	3.
	4. Set meeting schedule.	4.
5. Reward yourself.	1. Dinner at Mac's.	1. Amoco paid off
	2.	2.
	3.	3.

Chart 7.1 ■ DEBT SCHEDULE			
Lender	Amount Owed	Due Date	Payment Schedule

Chart 7.2 ■ LIVING EXPENSE SUMMARY			
	Amount Paid Monthly	Other Than Monthly	Total Annual Amount
Housing:			
Mortgage/Rent			
Insurance			
Property Taxes			
Electricity			
Heating			
Water			
Sanitation			
Telephone			
Cleaning			
Repairs/Maintenance			
Supplies			
Other			
Total Housing			
Food Total			
Clothing Total			
Transportation:			
Insurance			
Gas and Oil			
Repairs/Maintenance			
Parking			
Other			

Chart 7.2 ■ LIVING EXPENSE SUMMARY *(cont.)*			
	Amount Paid Monthly	Other Than Monthly	Total Annual Amount
Total Transportation			
Entertainment/Recreation:			
Eating Out			
Baby-sitters			
Magazines/Newspapers			
Vacation			
Clubs/Activities			
Other			
Total Enter./Rec.			
Medical Expenses:			
Insurance			
Doctors			
Dentist			
Drugs			
Other			
Total Medical			
Insurance:			
Life			
Disability			
Other			
Total Insurance			
Children:			

Chart 7.2 ■ LIVING EXPENSE SUMMARY *(cont.)*	Amount Paid Monthly	Other Than Monthly	Total Annual Amount
School Lunches			
Allowances			
Tuition			
Lessons			
Other			
Total Children			
Gifts:			
Christmas			
Birthdays			
Anniversary			
Other			
Total Gifts			
Miscellaneous:			
Toiletries			
Husband: misc.			
Wife: misc.			
Cleaning/Laundry			
Animal Care			
Beauty/Barber			
Other			
Total Miscellaneous			
TOTAL EXPENSES			

Chart 7.3 ■ CASH FLOW SUMMARY	
Gross Income:	$
Less:	
Giving	( )
Taxes	( )
Debt Payments	( )
Living Expenses (from chart 7.2)	( )
Cash Flow Margin:	$

Chart 7.4 ■ ACTION PLAN		
Step	**Action**	**Completion Date**
1. Determine where you are.	1.	1.
	2.	2.
	3.	3.
2. Stop going into debt.	1.	1.
	2.	2.
	3.	3.
3. Develop repayment plan.	1.	1.
	2.	2.
	3.	3.
4. Establish accountability.	1.	1.
	2.	2.
	3.	3.
5. Reward yourself.	1.	1.
	2.	2.

CHAPTER EIGHT

When Should You Use Credit?

B ob and Laura (a fictitious couple) have some typical problems to solve. They have three children, ages 8, 10, and 12. They live in a mid-western city of 100,000 people, attend a traditional church, and have two cars, a home mortgage, and the "normal" number of credit cards.

For years Bob and Laura have dreamed of the time when their children would be old enough to appreciate a month-long vacation at the beach. Next year Bob will have worked 15 years for his company, making him eligible for four weeks of vacation. Over the years they've saved whatever money they could in a vacation fund, and they now have $5,000. They estimate that to do what they want will cost all of that.

The children have increasingly been a part of this dream as they've grown, and they've even saved some spending money to be used when they go to the beach. Their plans are set, and the reservations have been made at a hotel that is the "ultimate" at "their beach."

A few weeks ago, however, Bob was talking to Fred, a long-time member of their Sunday school class and a good Christian friend, about the new business Fred is in. According to Fred, it's a part-time business and is "guaranteed" to provide $25,000 to $50,000 in extra income per year. It involves selling an oil additive to friends, family, and neighbors that greatly improves gas mileage. If you recruit others as salespeople, you can also earn a percentage of their sales. Fred has been in the business several months now and is so excited that he can hardly describe the tremendous opportunity this business represents.

When Bob relayed this conversation to Laura, she asked, "What does it cost to get into the business?"

Bob said it would cost them "only" $10,000 to buy the initial inventory and the franchise. Laura was really excited for Bob, because she's sensed for a number of years that he would like to do something on his own, and this may very well be the opportunity he's been yearning for. She had some strong reservations, however, about where they'd get the $10,000. She was also somewhat fearful of how much time it would take for Bob to make this business grow. But she kept her fears to herself and listened attentively as Bob explained everything.

The following week, Laura was driving the children to school in their four-year-old car when a teenage boy drove through a stop sign and demolished their car. Fortunately, no one was hurt, but the car can't be repaired, and now Bob and Laura need to replace it. The teenage boy had no insurance, and his parents couldn't help, either. When Bob checked his own insurance, he found he had neglected to buy uninsured motorist coverage.

As Bob now reviews their financial situation, he's thankful he has a good job he can count on. But with three growing children, there's not a lot of extra money. Their checking account balance is never more than $200 to $300 at the end of the month, and the only savings they have, other than the company retirement plan, is their vacation fund of $5,000. Bob and Laura have good credit, and they presently have no debt other than some small credit card charges and a loan on Bob's car.

Pete Andrews, a banker who attends the same Sunday school class as Bob and Fred, has assured Bob that if he needs to borrow money, his bank would be pleased to lend it. Pete has counseled Bob that it's wise to borrow in their situation, and he recommends they do so both to make the investment and to replace the car. He also assures Bob that if he needs a credit card to pay for his vacation, the bank would be delighted to extend that credit to him, too.

Bob and Laura are confused about what to do. They just attended a seminar on Christian principles of finance and came away thinking any kind of debt is wrong. Yet they've now been counseled by two Christian friends to borrow money to meet their "needs." How do they decide whether to borrow money? And if they do, should they borrow for the vacation, the car, the investment, or all three?

To answer these questions and to develop a framework for decision making when it comes to borrowing, let's look at debt in five categories. I'll then develop four rules to follow in making every borrowing decision. At the end of this chapter, we'll apply the four rules specifically to Bob and Laura's situation and consider what they should do. All this should equip you to apply the four rules to the borrowing decisions you're now facing or will face in the future.

FIVE KINDS OF DEBT

I can think of almost nothing that credit can't be used to fund. Giving to some ministries can be

Chart 8.1 ■ DEBT CATEGORIES			
Catagory	Normal Interest Rate	Term	Collateral
Credit Card	12%-21%	30 Days	Personal Guarantee
Installment	6%-14%	6-60 Mos.	Item Purchased
Mortgage	6%-15%	15-50 Years	Real Estate
Investment	8%-16%	Varies	Investments
Business	8%-16%	Varies	Assets of Business

done using credit cards. Groceries, furniture, and all forms of entertainment can be bought with them. Cars can be bought on time. Homes can be purchased—are almost always purchased—using debt. Even funerals can be paid for using some type of loan.

Our focus here, however, won't be so much on the purpose for borrowing money as on the kinds of debt incurred. The five categories we'll consider are distinguished by three factors:

1. the interest rate charged
2. the term (length of time) of the borrowing
3. the collateral required

The categories can be compared in chart 8.1 found on the preceding page.

Credit Card Debt

The distinguishing characteristic of credit card debt is that it carries a high rate of interest, generally no less than 12 percent and in many cases as high as 21 percent. The required repayment is either a minimum amount monthly or the full balance due each month. This debt typically requires no collateral other than personal creditworthiness.

Installment Debt

Installment debt is generally used to buy higher-cost items such as furniture, boats, or cars, and the item purchased is the collateral. The interest rate is typically less than that for credit cards but is still in the 6 to 14 percent range. The lender reserves the right to repossess whatever is financed should repayment fall behind schedule. The repayment itself is typically on a monthly basis over a period of time no longer than four or five years. This type of borrowing is promoted by the advertising phrase "easy repayment terms."

Mortgage Debt

Mortgage debt is typically used to purchase a home. Interest rates vary from time to time but are usually no more than 13 to 14 percent. Repayment is generally on a monthly basis for a period of no less than 15 years and in most cases 30 years. The distinguishing characteristic of home mortgage debt is that the collateral is the home or real estate purchased with the loan. We'll look at all forms of mortgage debt in chapter 12, including home equity loans.

Investment Debt

Investment debt is used to buy something with which you hope to make a profit. It may take the form of a multiple pay-in, as is typical in the purchase of tax shelters. More frequently, however, it's money borrowed from a lending institution. The interest rate is usually lower than credit card or installment debt, but it may be higher than mortgage debt. The repayment is almost always fixed over a relatively short period and may require fairly large payments compared to the other forms of borrowing. The collateral can be either a personal signature or, more likely, the investment itself.

In many cases, the temptation to use credit overwhelms both common sense and spiritual convictions. That's why there are objective rules to follow.

An example of investment debt is when people borrow using stocks they already own as collateral to buy additional stocks or bonds. This type of borrowing is called "buying on margin."

Business Debt
Business debt is borrowing done by a business rather than an individual. For example, a business may borrow to buy furniture, fixtures, and equipment; to expand its facilities; or to buy a building out of which to operate. It may also borrow just to increase its business in general terms.

A chief characteristic of this type of debt is that the interest rate varies with the credit-worthiness of the borrower, and the terms of repayment depend entirely upon negotiations between borrower and lender. This type of debt is almost always issued by lending institutions and is really their traditional function. Only since World War II have credit cards, installment debt, and mortgages become significant parts of their loan portfolios. Business debt is usually secured by the assets of the business or the personal guarantees of the owners for smaller firms.

There may be some overlap in these categories. For example, a business may buy a piece of property using a mortgage. For our purposes in the remainder of this book, however, any debt entered into by a business will be called business debt regardless of whether it has the characteristics of an investment, a mortgage, or even an installment purchase. There's nothing sacred about these categories, but I've found them to be easily understood and differentiated.

DECISION-MAKING RULES

I use four rules in making my own borrowing decisions, and I recommend them to you in making yours:

Rule 1: Common sense
Rule 2: A guaranteed way to repay
Rule 3: Peace of heart and mind
Rule 4: Unity

These rules don't necessarily make it easy to decide about taking on debt. The reason we even consider going into debt is to meet a need or desire that has become a high priority to us. In many cases, however, the temptation to use credit to meet the perceived need overwhelms both common sense and spiritual convictions. That's why there are objective rules to follow.

But rules by themselves will not cause right behavior. We must first choose to evaluate a borrowing decision relative to these rules. Then we have to *act* on the basis of that evaluation, which is the most difficult part of the process, because it may mean not having something you really want. On the other hand, choosing to act the way you believe you should will ultimately create a tremendous sense of satisfaction. Self-esteem goes up as you make right decisions.

Weighing today's desires against future benefits is a classic psychological definition of maturity. These rules, then, will help you to act maturely.

Rule 1: Common Sense
This rule can be stated as follows: For borrowing to make sense, the economic return must be greater than the economic cost. To state it another way, when money is borrowed, the thing it was borrowed to purchase should either grow in value or pay an economic return greater than the cost of borrowing.

Before I explain this rule, you should take the following test by putting a check mark in the appropriate column in chart 8.2 for each of the five kinds of debt.

Looking at this rule in reverse, it makes no

sense at all to borrow money if it's going to cost you more to borrow than what you're going to get in the way of an economic return. That return can be twofold. The thing purchased can grow in value, such as a home, or it can pay a return, such as a stock that pays dividends.

To ignore this rule is to say, in effect, that you're willing to borrow money and pay 12 percent interest in order to deposit it in a savings account earning 5 percent interest. I call this a commonsense rule because it makes no sense whatsoever to break it. Yet every day many people agree to rent money at a much higher cost than they can ever expect to receive in the way of an economic return.

A couple of things make it difficult to follow this rule. The first is the assumption that you can always earn more through your investments than what it costs to borrow money. If this assumption were true, you would always use

Chart 8.2 ■ RULE 1: COMMON SENSE		
	May Satisfy the Rule	**Will Never Satisfy the Rule**
Credit Card Debt		
Installment Debt		
Mortgage Debt		
Investment Debt		
Business Debt		

leverage. But with some forms of debt, such as credit cards or installment loans, such a rate of return is almost impossible to accomplish. This is one of the deceptions mentioned in chapter 4.

The other thing making it so difficult to follow this rule is that there is much false information and belief regarding some kinds of debt. For example, there's a general belief that houses *always* appreciate in value and that it therefore *always* makes sense to get into a home as quickly as possible using mortgage debt.

It's true that homes have generally appreciated in value over the last 40 years because of our inflationary economy. But it's also true that until the mid 1980s, it appeared that Texas, and specifically Houston, would continue to grow economically at a phenomenal rate due to increasing oil prices. When oil prices turned down in 1983–84, however, the whole economy turned bad in the Southwest, and home prices plummeted accordingly. Was that an aberration that will never occur in other parts of the country? Fortunately, I've lived long enough to know that there will be cycles in the economy regardless of where you live.

I well remember when the Northeast was very depressed economically and then became one of the hottest real estate areas in the country. Now, once again, it has softened considerably.

Atlanta in the early 1970s was an incredibly hot real estate market, with investors following what's called the "Greater Fool Theory." That theory says, "It doesn't make any difference what I pay for a piece of property, because there's a bigger fool than I am who will pay even more for it." Unfortunately, that didn't continue to be true, and many Christian (as well as non-Christian) investors consequently lost fortunes. Similar stories could be told about every section of the country.

Thus, history does not bear out the assumption that real estate will always increase in value. And if you have to sell at a time when the prices are down, it won't make any difference that in a few years they'll come back. You'll take your losses. One column in chart 8.2 is headed "*May* Satisfy the Rule" rather than "*Will* Meet It" because it's never certain prices will continue to go up.

Investment debt is also a complicated area to evaluate, because "there's no such thing as a bad investment. They only go bad." My firm probably evaluates a thousand investments per year. Each is presented to our investment department as a "good deal." No one has ever sent me a letter or asked to meet with me to show me a bad deal. Unfortunately, many investments "go bad"—but they weren't bad on the front end.

Investment debt, then, may meet rule 1, but it's never guaranteed to do so, even though every investment opportunity is presented as being such a good deal that it makes sense to use whatever means possible to take advantage of it. Not long ago, I counseled with a full-time Christian worker who had been presented with an "absolutely sure-fire" oil and gas investment by a Christian friend. This Christian worker had borrowed equity out of his home in order to invest. You can guess the end of the story. He invested $40,000, only to learn several years later that the investment was absolutely worthless.

It had been easy for him to borrow the money, but it was a real struggle to pay it back, as there was no economic return from the investment. The payments had to come from other potential uses of money, such as a college education for his children, giving, life-style desires, and so on.

Business debt is similar. If you own a company, it's extremely difficult to avoid, because your life is typically committed to your business, and that commitment clouds your judgment. It always seems that the opportunity justifies the borrowing. Consequently, many small business owners, and even large business managers, find themselves under such huge debt loads that the ultimate result is bankruptcy. Witness the Chrysler bankruptcy in the 1970s and the Eastern Airlines bankruptcy in the late 1980s (even though the company was generating more than $1 billion a year in revenue). They could not meet their debt obligations.

At the very least, when evaluating the borrowing decision regarding mortgage debt, investment debt, or business debt, you should do a thorough analysis of how the money will be used and the risk of not achieving the desired returns. A cold, hard look needs to be taken every time borrowing decisions are faced.

When it comes to credit card and installment debt, the economic return is never greater than the cost of borrowing. The interest rate is too high, and the items purchased or consumed by the use of that kind of debt never appreciate in value. Accordingly, those two forms of debt are almost never used by anyone attempting to meet rule 1.

Thus, the correct answers on chart 8.2 are that credit card and installment debt never meet rule 1, whereas mortgage debt, investment debt, and business debt may. But be very careful about assuming they'll absolutely satisfy it. Try to get all the facts, and make every effort to be objective. And at the very least, after you've done your analysis, you should believe that whatever you're getting ready to borrow for will provide an economic return greater than the economic cost. It only makes sense.

Rule 2: A Guaranteed Way to Repay
One of the biblical principles from chapter 5 is that debt always presumes upon the future. The

only way to avoid violating this truth when borrowing for any purpose is to have a guaranteed way to repay. For example, if you borrow money to buy a home and the lender is willing to take back the home as full payment of the debt in the event you're unable to pay, you have a guaranteed way to repay the debt. You're not presuming the continuation of favorable economic conditions.

Another example of consistency with this rule is the use of a credit card for convenience's sake. This morning I used my credit card to pay for some dry cleaning. I did this knowing the money was already in the bank to pay for that service. Using a card this way, strictly for convenience with the money in the bank, does not presume upon the future.

Many years ago, some partners and I had an opportunity to purchase a small bank. In evaluating whether the assets on the bank's books were good, we asked the officers some questions. We discovered they never made a loan unless the borrower had more money on deposit in the bank than the amount he wanted to borrow. Obviously, they didn't make a lot of loans. But they didn't have any loan losses, either.

The people who borrowed the money clearly had a guaranteed way to repay. This happened to be a farming community, and most of the loans were made to farmers who had certificates of deposit in that bank. They didn't want to cash in their CDs, but they needed working capital in order to plant the spring crop. Incidentally, because the crop would presumably be sold for more than what it cost the farmers to borrow the money, they didn't violate rule 1, either.

There are only three sources from which to repay borrowed money:

1. Income earned from sources other than that for which the money was borrowed.
2. The sale of whatever the money was borrowed for.
3. The sale or liquidation of some other asset, such as a certificate of deposit or savings account.

The reliability of that source of repayment depends on many factors. Only you, as the potential borrower, can make that evaluation.

Savings accounts, money market funds, stocks, bonds, or other assets that could be liquidated quickly are sure ways to repay (assuming, of course, that their value doesn't decline too much). The asset itself, such as a home, is a sure way to repay if it's worth more than the current loan balance. When you borrow 99 percent of the value of any asset, you have almost no protection against a drop in value. If, on the other hand, you borrow only 50 percent of the purchase price and you pay fair value for the home (or other asset), you have a reasonable assurance of being able to repay through the sale of the asset if it becomes necessary. Sometimes, however, assets can't be sold at any price because there are no buyers, such as when a region's economy is depressed.

Another way to keep from violating rule 2 is to have what is called an *exculpatory clause* in your loan contract. The word *exculpate* means "to vindicate or exonerate." Thus, an exculpatory clause literally means that the lender will exonerate you from having to repay the debt, taking back as *full* payment the asset that was used as collateral. There is, therefore, no personal liability. And there's no way you wouldn't be able to repay. It may be a costly and painful way to do it, but it does allow you to repay without presuming upon the future.

A last way to guarantee repayment of a loan is to have other assets set aside with which to pay it off if necessary. This is exactly what happened in the bank I described earlier. The farmers didn't need exculpatory clauses in their loan agreements, because the bank had taken as collateral sufficient assets to repay the debt.

All this means that if you're going to satisfy rule 2, you may not be able to borrow just when you'd like. You may not be able to make a significant down payment on a home, get an exculpatory clause inserted in the mortgage, or set aside sufficient assets to provide collateral for the loan. The question then becomes, do you go ahead and

Chart 8.3 ■ RULE 2: GUARANTEED REPAYMENT		
	How Is It to Be Repaid?	How Sure Is the Source of Repayment?
Credit Card Debt		
Installment Debt		
Mortgage Debt		
Investment Debt		
Business Debt		

borrow the money even though you'll be in violation of this rule? The answer is, not if you don't want to reject a biblical principle.

The best choices aren't always the easy ones, and it's at this point in the borrowing decision that faith calls you to act on the belief that God will meet your needs.

To summarize rule 2, chart 8.3 provides spaces for you to record how each type of debt is to be repaid and how sure is the source of repayment. When you complete this chart, be careful not to assume that everything is going to work out exactly as you would like. You need to ask yourself, *What if it doesn't work out the way I'm planning?*

If you don't have a guaranteed way to repay a debt you're thinking of assuming, by definition you would be presuming upon the future and taking the consequent risk of violating a biblical principle.

Rule 3: Peace of Heart and Mind

To determine whether you satisfy rule 3, you must ask yourself:

1. Why am I doing what I'm doing?
2. Does what I'm doing violate any scriptural principle?
3. Do I have peace in my heart, or spirit?
4. Do I have peace of mind when envisioning doing what I'm doing?

The first question gets at motives. Is the reason for borrowing to get rich quick, to avoid working, to satisfy a want, to give an appearance other than the truth, to meet a need, or to attain some other desire? This is a penetrating question to have to ask yourself. If you can become disciplined enough to ask it and answer honestly before every borrowing decision, at the very least it will cause you to delay making impulsive decisions. In most cases, it will keep you from borrowing for the wrong reasons. If you're unwilling even to ask yourself the question, the chances are pretty good your motives aren't right.

Another way to check your motives is to explain to your spouse or a good friend why you're doing what you're doing. Most of us are masters at deceiving ourselves so we can justify what we want to do. But when we have to explain our motives to someone else and it's unpleasant or uncomfortable, or if the borrowing "just doesn't sound right" to that person, our motives are most likely wrong.

After answering the first question, you almost always know the answer to the second. If the motive is wrong—greed, lack of discipline, lack of contentment—you know without having to find the scriptural reference that you're violating a biblical principle.

To illustrate the application of this rule, suppose a man could afford to pay $10,000 cash for a car, enough to buy a moderately priced new car or a nice used one. On the other hand, if he adds $15,000 of debt to this amount, he could drive a new luxury car. He may even be able to "afford" the payments on this luxury car. By asking himself, *Why am I considering going into debt to buy the luxury car?* he's challenging himself to examine his motives. If he's spending time regularly with God, praying and meditating on the Scriptures, he'll know if he's violating a biblical principle. God is faithful to lead us into the truth when we seek His will.

---

*Although their perspectives
are often quite different, a
husband and wife should be in
complete agreement regarding
borrowing decisions.*

I was in a jewelry store once having a ring sized, and I noticed a man buying a $2,500 watch. As I watched the clerk write up the sale, I saw that the man made a down payment with a credit card and arranged to pay the rest of the bill on an installment plan. He then put the watch on and walked out of the store. As far as anyone seeing him was concerned, he was a successful person because he was wearing a very expensive watch. Those who saw him would probably also assume he could afford it. But had he asked himself why he was borrowing money to buy a watch, he probably would have been embarrassed at his own motives, even if he weren't a Christian.

Regarding the third question, Colossians 3:15 says, "Let the peace of Christ rule in your hearts, since as members of one body you were called to peace. And be thankful" (NIV). When I read that verse, I envision a peace that surpasses human comprehension. It's the peace Christ exhibited throughout His early ministry, even when facing trials and temptations.

The verse says "let" that peace rule in your heart, much like an umpire who calls the balls and strikes in a baseball game. Such peace is the determining factor regarding whether you're living in accordance with God's will for your life. When that peace is missing, it's probably because you're running your own life as opposed to letting Christ be the ruler (or umpire). So when you consider a borrowing decision, you must have the peace of Christ ruling in your heart if you're to move ahead confidently.

Closely related to peace of heart is peace of mind. I would separate the two this way: The *mind* is the intellectual evaluation, whereas the *heart* is the spiritual and emotional evaluation. Our Lord does not have a cluttered or confused mind, and 1 Corinthians 2:16 declares that we have the "mind of Christ." Applying this to a borrowing decision, you should ask yourself, *Am I free from confusion about this? Do I have clear thinking and a solid conviction that this is the right decision?*

The questions related to this rule are not all-inclusive. They're meant to get you to examine your motives. The bottom line is, do you want what God wants?

Rule 4: Unity

I believe God puts men and women together in marriage to complement and fulfill each other, not frustrate and thwart each other. Yet many times in my own marriage, it seems difficult for my wife and me to communicate because we're coming at an issue from different directions. Our thinking processes and perceptions are different, and our backgrounds give us different insights. I'm sure we're not alone in this. I'm also sure it is God's intention to mold me into the image of Christ and to use Judy in that process (and vice versa).

Psalm 133:1 says, "How good and pleasant

it is when brothers live together in unity!" (NIV). This is a good biblical principle to follow when it comes to a borrowing decision. Although their perspectives are often quite different, a husband and wife should be in complete agreement regarding the choice. Both of them should have peace of heart and mind from following rule 3 when finally deciding to borrow. If either of them doesn't, they should not enter into the debt contract.

I don't understand it, but I know women have an intuitive sense about such decisions that men usually don't. I also don't know why my wife can see things clearly that I can't seem to see at all. But I do know that when I've listened to her out of respect for her insight—and even gone against what I felt to be right—I have avoided problem situations.

The rule of unity applies to all of a family's financial decisions, investments as well as borrowing. Specifically regarding investing, I have two rules for husbands: (1) if you can't explain it to your wife, don't do it; and (2) even if you can explain it to her and she understands, if she doesn't feel good about it, don't do it.

I was explaining these two rules to a group of professional athletes at a conference several years ago. As I spoke, I noticed one of the wives sitting in the back of the room with tears streaming down her face. I talked to her later and learned that her husband had retired from pro sports at age 40, having played on three world championship teams. He had ended his athletic career financially secure.

After he retired, he was approached about entering a business venture with some Christian businessmen. They wanted him to supply the capital, and they would supply the expertise. Against his wife's advice, he risked all they had accumulated on the deal. When that money was gone, he again ignored her counsel and borrowed to the point that eventually they lost everything when the business went bankrupt. Now here she was in middle age, married to a former professional athlete who had no marketable skills or expertise. And the whole situation could have been avoided had he heeded the two rules for husbands.

A commitment to unity between marriage partners (or, in the case of a single person, with an accountability partner) will help avoid most debt problems. But because accountability and unity go against our natures, it is the rule most often violated. Many men even consider it unreasonable. Their comment to me is, "You don't know my wife" or "You don't live with my wife." And of course they're right: I don't understand their wives. I don't understand my own wife many times!

But I do understand the truth of the Scriptures. God has put a husband and wife together to complete each other; the two are to become one. When I entered into marriage, I implicitly agreed that it was no longer "her way" or "my way" but now "our way." And a debt decision that I make can have tremendous impact not only on her *sense* of security, but also on her real security. Thus, I am obligated morally and ethically to make her a part of that decision.

I confess, however, that making my wife a part of financial decisions is no easier for me than it is for any other man. I can understand and even teach this truth on an intellectual basis, but on an emotional level, making my wife a part of the decision means I have to give up certain "rights."

Many times I haven't listened to my wife's counsel or even sought it when making significant financial choices, and each time I made a mistake. Recently, for example, I went ahead without her complete agreement and made a decision that cost us hundreds of dollars.

We had planned for the replacement of my car, and the amount we had budgeted would have allowed us to buy a nice used vehicle. While looking at cars, however, I found one I really wanted that cost $1,500 more than we had set aside. Against Judy's advice, I bought the car because it was such a "good deal." And that car has required more maintenance and repairs than any we've ever owned. It turned out that my car was made in the first year of that model, before the manufacturer had worked out all the "bugs."

Fortunately, we incurred no debt to buy the car. But I'm convinced that if I had listened to Judy's counsel, we would have bought a more sensible car and avoided a lot of headaches.

Russ Crosson's book *Money and Marriage* gives excellent advice on husband-and-wife communication skills regarding money.

APPLYING THE RULES

Let's return now to the situation of Bob and Laura with which we began the chapter. They were wondering whether to borrow money for an investment, a car, or a vacation, having only $5,000 available to cover all three "needs." As they evaluated what to do, they applied the rules in this chapter to each alternative. To borrow for the vacation, they would have to use credit card debt and pay it off over a long period. Therefore, rule 1, a return greater than the cost, was not met. They could, of course, use the $5,000 to pay for the vacation.

Buying a car using debt would require an installment note, which also would violate rule 1. A car depreciates in value and doesn't provide any type of economic return.

Borrowing to take advantage of the business opportunity may or may not meet rule 1. It would not meet rule 2, having a guaranteed way to repay, unless they used their $5,000 as collateral. If they were willing to mortgage their house to enter this business, rules 3 and 4 become critical. Bob must ask himself why he's willing to take on debt to do it. Is there any scriptural principle being violated? Does he have peace of heart and mind in making the decision? If he can come up with the right answers to these questions, the last question is, does Laura give her *full* support and agreement? If the answer is no, debt should not be used.

It's true that Bob and Laura need a car. So shouldn't they go into debt to get it? The answer is another question: Are they going to trust themselves by going into debt, or are they going to trust God by choosing the car over the vacation and waiting on Him to provide the vacation? As a creative alternative, they could take a lesser vacation than what was planned and buy a lesser car than they'd really like. In other words, split the $5,000 between the two. They may not like such a compromise, but the issue is believing that God's ways are the best and that He's responsible to meet the real needs.

You'll note that *choosing to follow these rules means Bob and Laura can't have everything they want.* They must give up something. That's true every time the decision is made not to take on additional debt. It may mean giving up a vacation, a car, a business opportunity, clothes, or something else you desperately want. But debt is an illusion promising "something for nothing" when the reality is that you *can't* have

Chart 8.4 ■ RULE 2: DEBT DECISIONS						
Borrowing Purpose	Kind of Debt to Be Used	Does It Meet Rule #				Decision
		1	2	3	4	
		Bob and Laura's Decisions				
Vacation	Credit Card	No				No
Car	Installment	No				No
Business	Business/Term Note	Yes	Yes (With a Home Equity Loan)	?	?	?
		Your Decisions				

something for nothing. These rules pinpoint that truth, helping you understand the costs and risks of borrowing.

The positive side of the decision not to borrow is that you're not putting yourself in a position that in the future could risk everything— your reputation, your family, all you've accumulated financially, and even your close walk with the Lord.

Chart 8.4 can help you evaluate each debt opportunity as it comes along. The first column asks you to list what that debt would help you to get. The second column is for the type of debt that would fund that desire. And the last columns are the rules we've gone over in this chapter, followed by a column for your decision.

I would encourage you to reread the rules so they become ingrained in your thought life to the point that you aren't even tempted to make a foolish debt decision. Let me say again, however, that I'm not asserting that borrowing money is a sin. Only the failure to repay is wrong. Following these rules will help you to avoid violating God's commandment to repay all debts. It will also allow you to live with a great deal of inner peace, as well as peace within your family.

CHAPTER NINE

Understanding Credit

My daughter Cynthia called from college to tell me she had received in the mail an unsolicited application for an American Express card. The accompanying promotional material said that as a college student, she already had a good credit rating. Her question to me was, "Dad, don't I need to have a credit card to get a good credit rating?"

Due to my vocation, she has grown up in a home in which money and money management are frequent topics of conversation. Yet she didn't have a clear understanding of debt and credit. If you've already read the first eight chapters of this book, you know more than she did at that point. But you may still be saying, "Why talk any further about the different kinds of debt? It appears that the use of debt doesn't make good sense except in very limited circumstances."

It's true that most of the common uses of debt don't make much economic or biblical sense. However, something as simple as cashing a check usually requires two forms of identification, one of which needs to be a credit card. We live in a society that forces us to use credit or to have good credit to transact the daily business of living.

The number of Americans who have absolutely zero debt throughout their lives is extremely small. Almost everyone has, or will have at some point, a home mortgage. In addition, every day you're confronted with the opportunity to borrow money for some purchase. It's essential, therefore, that you understand the different types of debt, the assumptions underlying them, and your own convictions regarding them to be able to respond wisely to the many offers to use debt.

Having a credit card does not cause one to go into debt.

I also feel strongly that parents and grandparents have the responsibility to train their children and grandchildren in the proper use of credit and debt. Children won't receive this training from anyone outside the home. It's not taught in schools or churches, and certainly not by peer groups. The home is the place where kids must get sound, consistent teaching.

Not only do most of us have some debt and

live in a society that compels us to have at least a working knowledge of credit and debt, but all of us, in the daily affairs of life, establish a credit record. Most of us seem to fear our *credit rating*, but it's really nothing to worry about when credit and debt are managed properly.

THE DIFFERENCE BETWEEN CREDIT AND DEBT

One of the primary points we need to understand is the difference between credit and debt. *Credit is having the right to borrow*. Credit deals with the potential borrower's integrity—his faithfulness and timeliness in paying his bills. Based on that integrity, a potential lender extends credit. That credit may require either the personal guarantee of the potential borrower, as with a signature loan, or collateral—some type of security interest in something of value, either the item purchased or another asset of the potential borrower.

Thus, credit is not the same thing as debt, but it's used to go into debt. Debt results when the credit extended is utilized for the purchase of some product or service. The Christian who believes that having credit cards is wrong should understand that having credit cards does not *cause* one to go into debt. It only means that credit has been made available to him. An individual's use, or misuse, of those credit cards causes him to go into debt.

The rest of this book focuses on the proper use of credit. But before looking at the specific borrowing opportunities and types of credit, we'll preview briefly how we're going to go about it.

OVERVIEW

It used to be that "being able to afford it" meant you could pay cash for whatever you were purchasing. If you didn't have the cash on hand, by definition you *couldn't* afford it. What a difference time makes! Today, "being able to afford it" has nothing to do with whether you have the resources to pay for it. It means strictly "being able to afford the monthly payments."

As such, every borrowing decision can be manipulated simply by extending the length of time of repayment in order to make it "affordable." Prior to World War II, home mortgages rarely went beyond 10 years. Today, 30 years is the standard, and in some cases it's possible to get a 50-year mortgage. Fifty years is probably longer than the buyer will last. But by extending the terms over half a century, the payments come down to the "affordable level."

This change in the way we view debt is one of its major deceptions. In chapters 3 and 4, we took a cursory look at the advertising deceptions and a detailed look at the financial deceptions. In the rest of the book, we're going to look at the deceptions of each individual type of debt so you can recognize them and make better, informed decisions regarding debt.

Debt-related deceptions are so effective because they make borrowing appear to be the wise and logical thing to do. For example, if you believe that "being able to afford it" means being able to afford the payments rather than being able to pay cash, you're certainly not equipped to resist the advertising that offers "easy payments." Nor will you consistently resist the advertising slogan proclaiming "no interest for 90 days."

Deceptions come from advertising, from salespeople, from financial counselors, and even from respected periodicals. Major portions of every weekly news magazine are devoted to money and money management, and many magazines are devoted strictly to those subjects—all of which generally perpetuate many of the borrowing deceptions. That's why it's critical to understand the deceptions relative to each kind of debt so we won't be taken in by them.

In addition to the deceptions, we will examine some of the legitimate questions and issues relative to each kind of debt. For example, just what is a credit rating, and how do you get and keep a good one? Should you buy credit life insurance? Is it better to buy or lease a car? Which type of home mortgage is best? Should college education be funded by a college loan? What does the term *APR* really mean? By addressing these questions, you'll be better equipped to make good debt decisions.

Lastly, in each chapter I'll give my recommendations regarding when and how to use that particular form of credit if it's appropriate to your situation. The recommendations are based on the assumption that you have already gone through the decision-making process outlined in chapter 8.

CHAPTER TEN

Credit Card Debt

"Marcia never gave much thought to how much she was spending with credit cards. 'My friends and I would go to the mall with our babies and spend the day just walking around,' says the easy-going thirty-three-year-old, who lives in a pleasant two-bedroom townhouse in a suburb of Chicago. 'I was always buying things ahead of time . . . a cute outfit my son could wear next summer; a toy on sale that I could put away for Christmas.

"'There was never anything major: Just clothes, meals, gas, birthday gifts—I put them on my charge. Truthfully, when I was charging I didn't feel like I was spending real cash.'

"Marcia takes off her designer glasses ('Charged, of course,' she says, grinning) and continues. 'My husband and I used to pay off our credit-card bills completely each year with our income tax refund, so we had a great credit rating, and every year the banks would offer us a higher limit. Our Visa started at five hundred dollars, and we got the limit up to thirty-five hundred. MasterCard was twenty-three hundred, and even after I got pregnant and quit my job, we were still invited to take out another MasterCard with a two thousand dollar line of credit. Then, of course, there was the Sears card, Montgomery Ward, Lord & Taylor, Marshall Field, Lerner, Wieboldt, Amoco, Shell, Union 76. . . . Oh, yeah, we also had a line of credit on our checking account for two thousand. It was great to know we could go out and get anything we needed anytime.'

"Marcia and her husband, Ted, are hardly unusual. Today about seven out of ten Americans use credit cards, totaling some 700 million accounts, according to the Federal Trade Commission.

Merely putting a credit card in a potential user's hand will lead the person to spend 34 percent more.

"There's no doubt that these ubiquitous pieces of plastic are a tremendous convenience. They enable people to travel without a great deal of cash, they minimize the trauma of robberies (reporting the crime immediately means you won't be held responsible for the thief's bills), they make record-keeping easier, and they allow people to live more comfortably. 'Credit is good for Americans,' says Luther R. Gatling, president of Budget and Credit Counseling Services of New York. 'It makes the quality of life better for everyone.'

"Yet Gatling readily admits that credit is a double-edged sword. Every year his agency sees hundreds of people who have gotten into serious trouble because of credit cards and loans. Financial counselors generally say that one out of six people who buy on credit is burdened by excessive debt. And all the advantages of credit are easily outweighed by the headaches and heartaches that accompany a mounting stack of unpaid and unpayable bills" (*Ladies' Home Journal*, April 1986, pp. 72, 178).

Marcia and Ted's situation, like Tom and Sue's (see chap. 4), is a classic illustration of how easy it is to fall into the credit card trap. And as the article telling their story points out, there are more than 700 million credit card accounts for a total population of approximately 240 million. That means there are nearly three credit cards for every man, woman, and child in the United States. If you assume that half the people don't have credit cards (because they're children), there are more than six credit cards per adult in America today.

Credit card companies aren't foolish, and they don't extend credit in order to lose money.

What they've found is that merely putting a credit card in a potential user's hand will lead the person to spend 34 percent more than if the individual didn't use that credit card. And because their losses will typically run no more than 5 percent of the outstanding balances, lenders can afford the risk of putting credit into the hands of those who are not credit-worthy. Charging an average of 18.86 percent interest, they much more than make up their losses from the millions of cardholders who pay their bills faithfully.

The *Ladies' Home Journal* article also said (and other sources corroborate this) that one out of six people who use credit is in trouble with debt. In other words, over 16 percent of all American families have a serious debt problem. To determine whether you have a problem with debt, answer the following true-false questions (taken from Sian Ballen, *Money*, April 1987, p. 96).

1. You spend money in the expectation that your income will increase in the future.
   True _____ False _____

2. You take cash advances on one credit card to pay off bills on another.
   True _____ False _____

3. You spend more than 20 percent of your income on credit card bills.
   True _____ False _____

4. You often fail to keep an accurate record of your purchases.
   True _____ False _____

5. You have applied for more than five credit cards in the past 12 months.
   True _____ False _____

6. You regularly pay for groceries with a credit card.
   True _____ False _____

7. You often hide your credit card purchases from your family.
   True _____ False _____

8. Owning several credit cards makes you feel richer.
   True _____ False _____

9. You pay off your monthly credit bills but let others slide, such as doctors' bills and utility bills.
   True _____ False _____

10. You like to collect cash from friends in restaurants and then charge the tab on your credit card.
    True _____ False _____

11. You almost always make only the minimum

payments rather than paying your entire credit card bill.

True _____ False _____

12. You have trouble imagining your life without credit.

True _____ False _____

Now score your responses. How many times did you answer true?

1–4 True. You can probably keep going. You don't splurge uncontrollably.

5–8 True. Slow down, you have entered the caution zone. It's time to draw up a budget, pay off your bills, and reevaluate your spending habits.

9–12 True. You have to stop. You might be wise to consult a credit counselor or financial planner for help in changing your spending habits.

MISCONCEPTIONS

People typically get into trouble with credit card debt because they fall victim to one or more popular misconceptions about credit. Their fall is hastened by the way these misconceptions appeal to our natural desires or fears, and by the fact that lenders aggressively promote this form of borrowing because they find it so profitable. I'm going to cover four of the most common misunderstandings here. Three of them are ones with which people delude themselves, and one shows how subtly we can be misled by this form of credit.

Misconception 1: You Can't Live Without It

We looked at the idea that "you can't live without it" as an advertising illusion back in chapter 3, but it bears reemphasizing here. This easily accepted notion accounts for a lot of credit card purchases. It also accounts to a large extent for why people who already have "enough" credit cards will apply for another they see advertised using that pitch. Credit cards are used exclusively, however, to buy temporal and depreciating items—nothing of any permanence. They're often used to pay for entertainment, which is certainly important to living a well-rounded life. But it's not the reason for our existence. People also use them, as one wag put it, "to buy things they don't need with money they don't have to impress people they don't know."

Always wait at least 24 hours to buy something you want after you first see it.

One way to avoid the unnecessary use of credit cards is to never make an impulse purchase. Always wait at least 24 hours to buy something you want after you first see it. That means you never buy anything the first time you go to a store unless it was already on your shopping list.

Following this procedure helps you think through what you want to buy and why. It allows the emotion of the impulse to fade and gives you a chance to consider how much you need the item and whether you really want to spend your limited dollars that way. If, after 24 hours and careful reflection, you still want the item enough to make a second trip back for it, you're more likely to be making a good decision.

Misconception 2: Having a Credit Card Means You're Credit-worthy

A second misconception is that because you're able to get a credit card, you must be credit-worthy. As pointed out earlier in this chapter, while credit card companies are concerned about credit worthiness, they're much more concerned about their profits. They're willing to take some significant losses while earning almost 20 percent in interest plus the fees they charge. Don't assume that just because you have a credit card, you can afford to take on debt. The test you took earlier should have highlighted for you whether you have a problem with credit cards. It's really scary, when you think about it, how easy it is to get approved on a credit card application. In some cases, it requires little more than your name, address, and telephone number.

Misconception 3: You Have to Have a Credit Rating

A third misconception is that you have a credit rating or you need a credit rating. *There is no such thing as a credit rating.* Various organizations compile credit reports on people who have used credit, but there's no single source to which anyone could go to get your credit rating. There's no scale that evaluates you in relationship to everyone else. Credit reporting agencies collect data regarding your credit history, payments, delinquencies, amounts borrowed, and so forth, but no central place gives you a credit rating.

The reality is that if you choose to avoid the use of credit cards because of following the four rules in chapter 8, then even if there were a credit rating, you wouldn't need it. A credit rating presumes there's risk associated with lending you money. But if you never borrow money this way, there's no risk and therefore no need for a credit rating.

Credit bureaus are nonprofit organizations that collect financial information on individuals from sources such as banks, retail stores, utilities, and other individuals. They maintain files on tens of millions of people. Those files are the source for the credit reports that most potential lenders use.

Establishing a good credit history is simple. Pay all your bills on time, and establish some banking relationships: that is, maintain checking and savings accounts. You don't need to borrow in order to have a good credit report.

Lending institutions are prohibited by the Equal Credit Opportunity Act from discriminating against anyone on the basis of sex, color, creed, religious preference, national origin, marital status, or age. Thus, anyone who's credit-worthy is entitled to receive credit.

Misconception 4: All Interest Is Equal

Another misconception is that there's no difference between an interest rate and an interest charge, when in fact there's a big difference. For example, suppose you borrow $1,000 at 12 percent interest for one year, with the full amount due at the end of 12 months. At that point you would owe $1,120. The interest rate and the interest charge would be one and the same, 12 percent.

However, suppose you borrow the same $1,000 at 12 percent, but instead of paying it back with one payment at the end of the year, you pay it back at the rate of $93.33 ($1,120 divided by 12 months) per month. The stated interest charge is 12 percent, but the *actual* interest rate paid is now approximately 21 percent, even though the total of interest dollars paid remains the same in both cases ($120).

The reason for this is that as you pay the $93.33 each month, you reduce the amount of principal you still owe by about $83. Yet you're still paying 12 percent interest on the full $1,000 throughout the year, even though the principal shrinks steadily from month to month.

Here's another way of looking at it. In the first case, a single payment at the end of the year, you have the full use of the $1,000 borrowed for the entire year. But in the second case, you have the use of only about $500 ($1,000 divided by two) for the full year, because you're paying back one-twelfth of the principal each month. The difference between borrowing $1,000 and paying $120 in interest and borrowing $500 (in essence) and paying the same total dollars of interest causes the big difference in effective interest rates. That's why the interest charge and the actual interest rate are two entirely different things.

One more way to understand the difference is to imagine that you borrow the $1,000 and immediately deposit it in a savings account. In the first case, that $1,000 can sit in the account and earn interest for you for the entire year. In the second case, however, over the course of the year you'll have an average of only $500 in the account to earn interest for you. Thus, the difference in effective interest rates on the two loans represents the opportunity you give up to earn money in the second case.

If you borrowed the $1,000 to buy a television set and a VCR, the salesperson would most likely tell you that was the "easy" way to pay for it. At only $93.33 per month, you could well "afford" it. But the fact is that while you could afford to take $93.33 plus interest out of your income each month, it was an extremely costly decision. Twenty-one percent interest, not many years ago, was considered usurious. Now it's considered normal for that type of purchase. This illustration graphically points out the deception of easy payments and the deceptiveness of interest.

Years ago, the government required all lenders to disclose to the borrower what is known as the APR, a uniformly calculated annual percentage rate of interest. The proper way to evaluate what it costs to rent money is to know the APR—the real interest rate the lender has charged and you have paid.

There are many superficial differences between credit cards. They charge different fees and interest rates and have various ways of calculating the interest rate. They have different repayment terms, and many offer attractive "come-ons." For instance, I recently received a signed $500 check in the mail from a credit card company. I could cash the check, and the amount would be added to my credit card balance. I could then "repay the $500 conveniently over many months." Other come-ons are free hotel rooms, frequent flier points, merchandise, and so forth offered to induce you to either accept or use the credit card. Just remember, however, that credit grantors are not benevolent. The enticement will cost you something.

RECOMMENDATIONS

Most of us are going to have to use credit cards at least occasionally to function in our credit card society. However, we *don't* have to use them to go into debt. There are three ways to get the benefits of using credit cards without going into debt:

1. Begin with a spending plan.
2. Use a debit card rather than a charge card.
3. Always pay the full balance at the end of the month.

Begin with a Spending Plan

My first recommendation is to begin with a spending plan. Unless you're operating according to that hated word, a *budget*, you'll never have any real reason to control your spending. To use credit cards to fund your living expenses is to invite temptation into spending decisions. As stated earlier, researchers have shown that you'll spend 34 percent more using a credit card than if you don't.

The way to use credit cards legitimately is for convenience only, staying within your spending plan and paying the balance in full when the bill comes. If you haven't already done so, set up an annual spending plan using the forms from chapter 7.

Use a Debit Card

My second recommendation is to use a debit card rather than a normal credit card. An amount charged to a debit card is immediately deducted from your bank or brokerage account balance. It's really no different from writing a check. My wife and I have a card that lets us earn interest on the total account balance until either a charge comes in or a check written against the account clears the bank. When we use the debit card, we enter the item in our checkbook just as if we had written a check. Then we deduct it from our available balance. In place of the check number in the check register, we put "VISA."

Using such a card allows you all the convenience advantages of a credit card, but you never have a credit card bill to pay because, in effect, it's paid the moment you use it. The only economic cost is the opportunity cost of not being able to "float" your purchases (i.e., earn interest on your money) for 30 days until the statement is received. But that's a small price for the freedom of never having a credit card statement to pay.

Always Pay the Full Balance

My third recommendation is that for regular charge cards, you never allow a month to go by without paying off the full balance. If you're tempted not to pay the full amount because it will make a big dent in your available cash, you're not using the card properly. A credit card can be a great convenience, but it should never be used to go into debt. Credit card debt violates the first rule in chapter 8. The cost of credit card debt—12 to 21 percent interest—is always greater than the economic return of whatever the card was used to buy.

Burn Your Credit Cards
My final recommendation is that if you can't follow the suggestions above, or if the earlier test shows you have a problem with credit cards, destroy them as I proposed in chapter 7. Make yourself a colorful decoration that can be hung on your refrigerator as a visual reminder of your problem, and you'll never be tempted to use those cards again.

By the time the credit card companies send you unsolicited replacements, your spending patterns should be reset and the addiction to the use of credit cards broken.

CHAPTER ELEVEN

Installment Debt

A newly married couple was visiting in our home, and the young man asked me if we could discuss a problem he had. His father-in-law was extremely angry with him because he had decided to sell the car that had been a "gift" from the father to the daughter. The new husband thought he was making a wise financial choice, but his father-in-law's response had shaken him.

The father had wanted to give his daughter a nice sports car, but this is how he did it: He made the down payment on the car *and then handed the young woman the coupon book requiring car payments of more than $300 per month.* While the daughter was single, those payments weren't much of a problem. When she married this young man—a missionary—however, the car payment added to their other expenses was more than their monthly income.

As the new husband evaluated their budget, he concluded that they could keep the car or their apartment, but not both. Thus his reasonable decision to sell the car. But this explanation was unacceptable to his father-in-law because he felt he had made a gift of that car to his daughter.

I thought, *What a tragedy that a father would make a gift of a payment book to his daughter!* I've since discovered that such is a common way of "giving" children a car, and it's another example of how completely debt-oriented our society has become. Almost 20 percent of the disposable income of most American families goes toward the retirement of consumer debt, of which installment debt is the largest portion.

Many times people tell me they don't have any debt, yet when I ask if they have a mortgage, they say, "Oh, yes." Then I ask if they owe on their car. They again say, "Oh, yes." The point is that most people don't even think of installment debt as debt. And those who pay cash for cars, trucks, boats, furniture, and other expensive items are rare. When you do pay cash for a car, as I recently did, the price may go *up* because the dealership doesn't get to earn interest from lending you the money (or a commission from referring you to a bank).

In this chapter, we're going to look briefly at a couple of deceptions related to this type of borrowing, discuss an important principle called "the opportunity cost of consumption," and then deal extensively with the purchase of an automobile, which is the most common use of installment debt. I'll also tell you about the cheapest car you'll ever own.

DECEPTION 1: IT MAKES MORE SENSE TO BORROW THAN TO PAY CASH

One time several years ago, I was flying home from California and had picked up the *Los Angeles Times* before leaving the airport. I was intrigued by a financial article that really seemed to make sense. It told about a psychology professor who had saved to pay cash for a new car but who had been told by the salesman that he would come out ahead financially if he put his money in a certificate of deposit paying 8 percent and financed the car with a loan costing 14.2 percent.

The professor's understandable initial reaction had been, "You just don't believe it. It's counter-intuitive: Anyone can see 14 is bigger than 8." Then he added, "When you've just spent several hours nickel-and-diming with an auto dealer, you're not inclined to jump when they say they have another good deal for you."

But that night, the professor couldn't sleep, so he went to his computer and did the calculations himself. As he worked out the numbers on different options, he concluded that if he took the 14.2 percent loan, he'd break even with just a 7 percent return on his investment. If he could earn 10 percent, he'd make almost $1,500 more than he paid out over the four years of the loan.

Calculating both the cost of the loan and the investment earnings month by month, the professor could also see that the deal worked so well because the 14 percent is charged against a *declining* balance, whereas the 8 percent is paid on a *growing* balance. "Generally speaking, 'an easy rule of thumb is if you can earn an interest rate equivalent to half the interest rate of your loan, you'll come out ahead,' says Frank Sperling, vice-president at Security Pacific National Bank" (*Los Angeles Times*, September 23, 1985).

Not long after returning to Atlanta, I was speaking with one of my employees about paying cash for a car versus financing it. A friend had just given him the illustration outlined in chart 11.1. It seems to show clearly that if someone has the cash to pay for a car, it pays to keep the cash and finance the purchase. Both the newspaper column and this illustration seem to make sense. One piece of advice came from an independent columnist who has no reason to mislead anyone. The second came from a salesperson at an auto dealership, but he used a computer to do the calculation, and as we all know, computers don't lie.

Both examples seem to prove mathematically that debt is advantageous. But there is one alternative neither person considered, and that's to use the cash to pay for the car. Then, instead

Chart 11.1 ■ PAY CASH OR FINANCE		
Cost of Car	$15,000	
Cash in Bank	$15,000	
Payments on Car Loan	$395 per month for 48 mos.	
Interest Rate	12.00%	
CD Savings Rate	9.00%	
Dealer's Analysis		
$15,000 Invested at 9% for 48 Mos. Grows to		$21,174
Original Investment		$15,000
Interest Income		$ 6,174
Total Payments on Car Loan ($395/mo. x 48 mos.)	$18,960	
Original Amount Borrowed	($15,000)	
Interest Expense		($ 3,960)
Advantage of Financing		$ 2,214

of making a monthly loan payment, you make the monthly payment to yourself and deposit it in an interest-bearing account. Chart 11.2 shows the result.

The gain is $2,381 if cash were paid for the car and a monthly payment of $400 were made to yourself and invested at 9 percent, as opposed to keeping the cash and financing the car as recommended by the salesman and the columnist. If you assume their motive was to tell the truth, they

Chart 11.2 ■ ADVANTAGE OF PAYING CASH		
Investment Value of a Monthly Savings of $400 that Earns 9% for 48 Months		$22,842
Taxes Paid on Interest Earned		($ 1,043)
Net Investment		$21,799
True Investment Value from chart 11.1		
Future Value of CD	$21,174	
Taxes Paid on Interest Earned.[1]	($ 1,756)	
Net Investment		$19,418
Advantage of Paying Cash		$ 2,381

1. The difference in taxes is due to the difference in average principal actually invested. One begins with a large principal amount; the other grows over time.

actually told a half-truth. It is *always* financially advantageous to pay cash for a car and save the monthly payment, literally as well as figuratively.

The only time this wouldn't be true is if the interest rate charged by the lender dropped to about half the rate that could be earned through investment. If the lending rate ever drops that low, however, the dealer is assuredly making up the lost interest by charging a higher price for the car. In that case, you'd still be better off paying cash for the car and negotiating the price down accordingly.

I've never found an alternative better than paying cash for a car. Because it's a depreciating item, borrowing to buy it violates rule 1 of our guidelines. Many times someone will say to me, "Well, I can't afford to pay cash." In that event, the answer is simple: "You can't afford that car."

If you can't afford to save in order to pay cash, you can't afford to buy on credit.

A money maxim summarizes the situation well: "If you can't afford to save in order to pay cash, you can't afford to buy it on credit." This is true because the cost of credit will always be more than the "cost" of savings. If you delay saving, thus believing you're forced into buying on credit, you won't be able to afford the payments any more than you could afford to save.

DECEPTION 2: EASY PAYMENTS

The second common deception with installment debt is the idea of "easy payments." There's no such thing. Again, if you can't afford to save, you can't afford to make payments. Payments *appear* to be easy only when you extend the term of repayment. Car loans used to be made for 24 months. Now they're commonly extended to 48 or even 60 months. As prices go up, the length of repayment becomes longer. Notice, too, that interest rates don't drop with longer-term loans; they also continue to rise.

THE OPPORTUNITY COST
OF CONSUMPTION

Assume that you borrow $10,000 to buy a car and pay off the loan over four years. During those four years, you have an average amount borrowed of approximately $5,000 (the principal balance owed declines as you make payments). Further assume that you continue to borrow $10,000 every four years in order to replace your car throughout a working life of 40 years. You have thus borrowed an average of $5,000 for 40 years.

The golden rule: "He who has the gold, rules."

Now assume that the average interest rate you pay is 12 percent. Looking at chart 11.3, come down the left-hand column to 40 years, then find the 12 percent column across the top. At the point where the two columns intersect, you see a factor of 93.1. That factor multiplied times $5,000, the average amount borrowed, computes to $465,500. This is the amount the lender has earned by collecting your interest

Chart 11.3 ■ THE OPPORTUNITY COST OF CONSUMPTION							
Years with Auto Loan	Loan Interest Rate						
	8.0%	10.0%	12.0%	14.0%	16.0%	18.0%	21.0%
5	1.5	1.6	1.7	1.9	2.1	2.3	2.6
10	2.2	2.6	3.1	3.7	4.4	5.2	6.7
15	3.2	4.2	5.5	7.1	9.3	12.1	17.5
20	4.7	6.7	9.6	13.7	19.5	27.4	45.3
25	6.9	10.8	17.1	26.5	40.9	62.7	117.4
30	10.1	17.5	30.1	50.6	85.9	143.4	304.5
35	14.8	28.1	52.7	98.1	180.3	328.1	789.8
40	21.7	45.3	93.1	188.9	378.7	750.4	2048.4

and reloaning it to someone else at 12 percent.

To state it conversely, if you saved your money in an account earning 12 percent compounded interest, you have to make only an initial deposit of $5,000 and leave it untouched for 40 years to have the $465,500 the lender has earned at the end of that same period. (This illustration ignores the tax impact of both interest deductions and interest income, but the point is still valid. It also assumes your interest would be compounded annually; if compounded more often, as is usually the case, your earnings would be a lot higher—e.g., $566,143 with quarterly compounding.) Thus, when you choose to borrow rather than save, you're giving up the opportunity to earn. That opportunity given up is what I call the "opportunity cost of consumption."

You can do your own calculations using the chart to see what you're likely to give up (or maybe have already given up) when you borrow. Think about it. Would you rather be a borrower or a saver (lender)? I'm reminded of the golden rule: "He who has the gold, rules."

TRANSPORTATION OR SIGNIFICANCE?

Three topics need to be addressed regarding the buying and selling of cars. (1) Why buy a particular car? (2) When to replace? (3) How to pay for the replacement?

Why Buy a Particular Car?

It's rare to find a family that doesn't have at least one car. And some families have three, four, five, or even six. The need for cars is obvious. Our family lives in Atlanta, Georgia, where the dilemma is that it takes at least 30 minutes to get anyplace. All the roads and interstates seem to be under continual repair or construction.

As a consequence, getting around is extremely time-consuming. It's not at all uncommon for a mother with school-age children to spend several hours a day in her car getting them to and from school and extracurricular activities. Businessmen going to and from work can easily spend an hour a day in their cars.

So when our oldest daughter was about to turn 16, I realized I could save my wife many hours per week if I bought our daughter a car and allowed her to do a portion of the carpooling to and from school. The question to me was not "Should a 16-year-old have a car?" but "How can I best meet the transportation needs of my family?" My daughter is a responsible young lady, but I purchased the car and loaned it to her for *our* convenience.

There's only one real reason people should buy cars, and that's to provide transportation. Our daughter was delighted by the opportunity to drive. Even though we provided her with an older, inexpensive "tank," she's been more than happy to drive it for the last several years because it gets her safely where she wants to go.

The point is that all the "bells and whistles" that go along with cars are nice but certainly not necessary. They're luxuries. Whether you're willing to pay for them comes back to what you're really trying to do in buying a particular car. If you're searching for significance or you lack discipline or contentment as described in chapter 2, you may make foolish economic decisions.

When to Replace?
In 1972, I was a fairly successful businessman. Not yet a Christian, I was seeking all the trappings

of success, but because I was only 30 years old, I chose to buy an Oldsmobile 98 rather than a Cadillac as my first new car. My reasoning was that it would be a few years before I was old enough and "mature enough" to look right driving an expensive luxury car. The Olds 98 actually had all the luxury features of the more expensive car, but it didn't have the Cadillac aura.

Two years after I bought the car, I became a Christian. Many things about my life changed, particularly the value system under which I operated, and in the late 1970s, I moved my family to Atlanta to enter full-time ministry work. By the early 1980s, the Olds 98 had over 100,000 miles on it and was still running fine. It looked terrible, however. It had become rusted. The vinyl top peeled. The power seats and windows didn't work all the time. The seat fabric was worn through. The car generally just did not give a favorable impression. Therefore, I began looking around to replace what had become known affectionately as "Old Blue."

Being an accountant, I assumed I would be able to analyze a new car purchase and come up with absolutely the most economical replacement. Smaller foreign cars had become quite popular, often getting 30 to 50 miles per gallon; Old Blue got only eight or nine miles per gallon. The cost of repairs and maintenance had also gone up on Old Blue.

I spent months evaluating the car alternatives. And the conclusion I finally reached amazed me: the unhappy and unwanted fact was that the cheapest car I could own was the car I already had. I extended my evaluation using all types of purchase scenarios, and in every case the cheapest car I could own was Old Blue. Over the years, I've also evaluated other people's car-buying options, exploring all the opportunities, and in every case I had to conclude that the cheapest car they could own was the car they presently had.

Your current car is the cheapest because even though many costs go up the longer you own a car, many others go down. An article in *Money* magazine titled "The Case for Hanging on to Your Aging Family Car for 100,000 Miles" said the following: "The considerable financial advantage of hanging on to a car for at least eight years has been demonstrated by Runzheimer International of Rochester, Wis., a worldwide transportation consultant to corporations. Runzheimer's analysts posed two choices last year for the owner of a mid-size, six-cylinder 1984 Chevrolet Celebrity, then four years old and free of debt: drive it another four years or trade it in on a 1988 model and drive that car for the next four years.

"The main finding [shown in chart 11.4] was that by sticking with his '84 Chevy, the owner would stand to save $5,036 despite the analysts' estimate that in four years of steady driving (60,000 miles), repair costs for the older car would exceed those of the new car by $1,179 and that the '84 model would consume $428 more gas and oil.

"There are, however, offsetting economies. One is modestly lower insurance premiums on an older car. As an auto loses trade-in value, you pay less to insure it for theft and collision damage. But the lost value, together with financing costs, is what knocks the new car out of contention. Those two items would be expected to account for nearly 55% of the total costs of keeping an '88 Celebrity on the road during its first four years of life. On the debt-free '84 model, depreciation would total just 35% of expenses. And in this regard, a Chevy is no different from a Ford, Cadillac or Mercedes" (*Money*, March 1989, pp. 165–66).

The analysis in this chart, done by an independent, worldwide transportation consultant, bears out what I had discovered several years earlier. How often have you used, or heard used, these reasons for trading in a car:

1. "My car is now approaching 50,000 miles, and that's a good time to trade, because the car loses value so quickly after that point."
2. "Three to four years is the best time to trade."

Both reasons are really justifications; *they are not borne out by any economic study*. There are,

Chart 11.4 ■ FOUR-YEAR COST OF OWNERSHIP	Old Car	New Car
Loan Payments (Interest & Principal)	$ 0	$10,166
Gas and Oil	3,428	3,000
Insurance	2,213	2,403
Repairs, Maintenance, and Tires	2,562	1,383
Total Expenses	8,203	16,952
Trade-in value	924	4,637
Net Cost of Ownership	7,279	12,315
Saved by Not Trading In	5,036	
Source: Runzheimer International		

however, three legitimate reasons for replacing a car, and they have to do with time, repairs, and safety.

Time. When a car requires so much of your time in keeping it repaired that the cost of your time is greater than the cost of replacing the car, it should be replaced. If my wife is spending two or three days a week with her car in the shop and is therefore using my car or going without transportation, at some point the cost of our time is such that it becomes wise to replace the vehicle. It may still be more economical from a straight dollars-and-cents standpoint to keep and repair the old car, but the cost in time is too great.

People who depend on their cars for their livelihood (e.g., salespeople, real estate agents) also have to consider the cost of time. If their cars are unavailable one or two days a week because of repairs or maintenance, it makes sense to replace them and get back that one or two days of productive time.

Only you can put a value on your time and determine if keeping your old car is costing too much. Obviously, time spent in the repair shop is time you can't spend on other activities, including those that generate income. But valuing your time can be a highly subjective exercise. I would encourage you, therefore, if you think your cost in time validates a decision to buy a new car, to talk it over with your accountability partner.

Cost of repairs. The second reason for replacing a car is excessive repair costs. Determine if the cost of needed repairs is greater than what the car will be worth after it's fixed. This typically doesn't happen until well over 100,000 miles or 10 to 12 years of driving the vehicle.

Safety. The third legitimate reason to replace a car is that it has become unsafe. This judgment may depend as much on reliability as anything else. For example, I would never want my wife or daughters to take the risk of becoming stranded at night along the road. Obviously, saving money is not the overriding consideration when you're concerned about your family's safety.

Be careful in using any of these three reasons for making the decision to replace your car. They're legitimate reasons, but don't use them to kid yourself. Is your plan to replace a car really a root problem as we discussed in chapter 2, or do you have a valid reason?

Often when I speak to groups on this topic, it's at this point that someone raises a hand and asks what kind of cars I have. You might assume from my recommendations that I drive 15-year-old, 200,000-mile cars regardless of their appearance. And you might assume I force my wife and children to do the same. I jokingly answer that question by saying I have a Mercedes and two BMWs. Please be assured that's not the case, but neither is the first perception true. Our cars are decent vehicles, only one of which was purchased new.

I, like you, want to drive a nice car. I can identify with those who love to drive a new car because "it smells so good." There are few things so satisfying, so appealing to your sense of pride and self-fulfillment, as to be able to drive a new car off the lot for the first time. Some men relish it so much that they trade for new cars more than once a year. Others never will experience the feeling because they have the discipline not to fall into that trap.

My counsel to those who are particularly susceptible to the temptation to replace cars prematurely is to always pay cash. When I suggest that, people generally respond, "I can't afford that." And to me that answers the question of whether it's time for them to replace their cars.

How to Pay for the Replacement?

I well understand the temptation to buy more car than you can afford. I even believe there are times when it's OK to buy a car that's more than you need in terms of basic transportation. And there are three issues to consider when it comes to funding the replacement:

1. New versus used
2. Lease versus buy
3. Cash versus borrow

New versus used. In almost every case, it will be less expensive to buy a used car rather than a new one, providing you do a good job of shopping the alternatives. Frequently the reason given for purchasing a new car is that you won't be buying someone else's problems. But new cars break down, too. What you're really looking for is a reliable car that will get you where you're going.

Proper shopping can help you find a good used car. Never buy one without first taking it to a mechanic to have it checked. Also examine the service records of the previous owner to determine the kind of care the car has received. Assuming you can satisfy yourself that the car you're buying is in good shape, a used car will always be the wisest economic choice.

Buying a new car can be a legitimate decision, however, if you follow two rules. The first is that you plan to drive the new car for at least eight to ten years. That way the heavy early depreciation of the car is irrelevant, because you will have spread out the total depreciation over that lengthy time period. The second rule is that you pay cash for the new car. As has been proved already, it is always more advantageous economically to pay cash rather than borrow. This is never more true than in buying a new car.

Paying cash generally causes you to make a better decision than you would if you borrowed. It's much easier to borrow $10,000 to $15,000 because you have "easy payments" of $250 per month than to write a check for $15,000. Somehow it's difficult to part with money that has been hard earned and hard saved. And that's exactly why I recommend always paying cash for a car, especially a new one.

Every major purchase, in fact, should be made with cash. It's even helpful (though I've rarely seen it done) to go to the bank and draw out the money in large bills. That helps you focus on the reality that you've traded off a part of your life to earn that money so you can now have whatever it is you desire so strongly.

Lease versus buy. Recently I heard a commercial from a luxury auto dealership here in Atlanta that basically said, "You can probably drive much more car than you think you can."

The salesman promised that through either their financing program or their leasing program, he could put you in a foreign-made luxury car you didn't think you could afford (with good reason). Once again the deception of "easy payments" was being used to appeal to consumers. The lease-versus-buy decision, which is becoming more and more common, preys on this deception. Absolutely the *only* economic benefit to leasing is that in most cases the payments are less than comparable financing payments.

The leasing decision, however, will *never* be more advantageous than financing, let alone paying cash. A lease is set up strictly for convenience. The lessor (car dealer) allows the lessee (customer), within limits, to set up his own convenient lease plan. All the lessor does to make it work for the lessee is to adjust the time period of the lease and/or the back-end replacement cost the lessee must guarantee (more on this below).

In calculating how much to charge on a lease, the lessor does the same calculations you should do when buying a car. He determines what his actual cost is going to be depending on the terms you want; he adds to it the financing cost he's going to bear (dealers buy their inventory on credit); and then he adds on his profit margin. All he's really doing is giving you the ease of making one payment rather than taking the multiple responsibilities of ownership. You can put the license plates and insurance in the lessor's name.

Repairs and maintenance can be handled by the lessor. But for that convenience, the lessor charges you all those costs plus his profit margin. It is never economically advantageous to lease. At best it can only be more convenient.

Two arguments are given for leasing even when it's clear you pay a premium to do so. One is that it's easier to take a tax deduction for a business car by leasing rather than buying. The other is that it's more convenient to replace the car because you don't have to sell it at the end of the lease.

However, if you can meet IRS requirements for deducting a lease payment, you can certainly qualify to deduct the costs of owning a car. Those costs are depreciation, repairs and maintenance, parking, tolls, and so on. The determining factor for the deductibility of a car is not whether it's leased or purchased, but whether it's used for business purposes. Leasing has nothing to do with tax deductibility.

It's true that with a lease you can replace your car at the end of three, four, or five years merely by turning it in for another leased car. However, there's a cost associated with doing so. The lessor will require you to guarantee his back-end value on that car. When you turn it in, if the actual value is less than the originally estimated value (because of depreciation, high mileage, or the condition of the car), you pay the difference in cash.

Additionally, you're paying the lessor a premium to do something you can do yourself: sell the car or trade it in. If you've followed the "new versus used" rules above, you'll be driving it for at least eight to ten years anyway. And to say that it's more convenient to lease because of the trade-in or replacement aspect is to say that you prefer to be what the Bible calls "slothful." It's also shortsighted and foolish.

If you gather that I feel strongly about the deception of leasing versus buying, you have interpreted correctly. Leasing is convenient, but it is *never* necessary.

Cash versus borrow. By now you know my recommendation on the cash-versus-financing alternative. But if you're feeling a need to replace a car now and you don't think you can afford to pay cash, let me close this chapter by showing you a way to be able to pay cash for your cars.

Let's assume you have a $1,000 repair bill facing you on your car, which is why you think you should trade. If you spend that $1,000 now and then save $100, $200, or $300 per month in a savings account earning 6 percent, you'll have one of the amounts shown in chart 11.5 at the end of whatever time period you choose.

If, instead of spending $300 per month on car payments, you put that amount in savings and wait one year, you can have a $3,698 car (less taxes on the $98 interest) for which you could pay cash. It's true you won't be driving the same luxury car that $300 per month could buy. But it's also true that you won't have the installment debt. If you continue to save the $300 per month, three more years later you'll have another $11,773 (less taxes on the interest), and then you can upgrade to a car costing that amount. If you keep that car for just four years, you'll have saved $16,177 (less tax) more to buy the next new car.

You can see from this chart that the longer you save to buy the car, or the longer you drive the car you now have and make the payments to yourself, the more car you'll be able to afford later. This again illustrates the value of delaying gratification of your desires, as well as the truth of our maxim "If you can't afford to save for it, you can't afford to borrow for it." If the money is available to make payments, the money is also available to be saved. All you

Chart 11.5 ■ **SAVE TO BUY**			
Amount in Fund at the End of Year (Before Taxes) if Amount Saved Per Year Is:			
Year	$100/Mo.	$200/Mo.	$300/Mo.
1	$1,233	$2,465	$3,698
2	2,539	5,079	7,618
3	3,924	7,849	11,773
4	5,392	10,785	16,177

have to do is delay making the decision to buy until later.

Apart from understanding and solving the root problems described in chapter 2, however, you won't be able to make this kind of decision. There will always be justifications for making poor decisions. There will always be an advertiser, a salesperson, or a friend to point out some great-sounding deal. But as I've said before, "If it sounds too good to be true, it probably is."

All this counsel is really a call to return to the way our parents and grandparents lived. We would benefit greatly from getting back to their definition of "being able to afford it," which is that you can afford to pay cash.

Old-fashioned? Yes.

Revolutionary? That would be great.

CHAPTER TWELVE

Mortgage Debt

Judy and I used to teach a young marrieds' Sunday school class, and one of the first Sundays we taught, we asked the group to name some of their personal goals and objectives. We had a spirited conversation that was finally summarized by one young man who said that most of them expected to start financially where their parents had left off after 25 to 40 years of hard work. They wanted to have two cars and a three- to four-bedroom home in a nice area that was close to work. They also wanted the home to be fully furnished when they moved in.

Judy and I had to laugh in private afterward. We've been married 28 years at the time of this writing, and our home still isn't fully furnished as we would like. We have no major wants, but it's taken us this long to get where we are today. I expect that about the time we finally finish decorating, we'll want to move into a much smaller home.

I find in talking with young couples that the

biggest problem they face is unrealistic expectations. This is typified by the home purchase
decision. It is probably the most significant
financial decision any married couple will ever
make, and there are four realities with which
young couples need to align their expectations.

First, unless they have financial help from
relatives, a new house or a house right after
marriage may very well be out of reach. The
average price of a house is so high that it's difficult for any couple, let alone a young couple, to
afford one unless they both work or are willing
to overextend themselves financially.

Owning a house is not a right, but a privilege.

Second, owning a house is not a right, but a
privilege. When it's viewed as a privilege, the
appreciation of ownership is much greater
when it's finally achieved. When something is
perceived as a right, however, there is a high
level of frustration if that "right" seems an
impossibility.

Third, purchasing a home will require financial sacrifices in some other part of the budget.
There are many ancillary costs of home ownership that aren't usually taken into account
because they're unknown. But the money for

repairs, taxes, replacement of appliances, and so on has to come from somewhere.

Fourth, God can be trusted to meet our needs. He won't necessarily meet our wants, but without question He will meet our every legitimate need. And while everyone has a need for shelter, that doesn't necessarily mean a house, and certainly not a dream house. Many times God will withhold a blessing until it can be given in such a way as to demonstrate His faithfulness, goodness, and trustworthiness.

In this chapter, we'll first look at some of the common misconceptions concerning buying and owning a house. Next we'll examine some common issues: the best type of mortgage, home equity loans, refinancing, paying off a mortgage early, equity sharing, and credit life insurance. Then we'll go over some helpful hints that appear to provide a "free lunch."

COMMON MISCONCEPTIONS

The first misconception that needs to be dealt with has already been pointed out—that owning a home is a right. No one has a right to a house. Home ownership is part of the American dream, but it certainly isn't a right. When and if God chooses to provide a house, that's a privilege. I'm disturbed, frankly, by the selfish, short-term attitude expressed by many young Christian couples. One of my desires in writing this book is to help young couples face reality so they won't try to borrow themselves into the illusion of prosperity. Going into debt for cars or houses should be avoided unless it's clearly the best financial alternative.

Believe me, I understand the strength of the desire for a house that young couples feel, and I confess I haven't always followed the principles I now know should govern the house-buying decision. When Judy and I bought our first home in 1968, we paid $25,000 for a four-bedroom, two-bath brick home in the northern suburbs of Dallas, Texas. We borrowed the 5 percent down payment from my parents and financed the other 95 percent with a 30-year, 7 percent fixed-rate mortgage. That home is now, most likely, worth substantially more than $25,000.

In retrospect, our decision to borrow to buy looks good because of the appreciation and because we got a low fixed rate. But the financial risks to a young couple are greater today: jobs aren't as secure as they used to be; appreciation is by no means guaranteed, as Texans know well; and fixed-rate loans at such low rates are rarely available. To put it simply, I would never finance a home today the way I did it back in 1968, and I wouldn't have done it then if I'd known the facts I'm giving you in this book.

A second misconception is that what was true is always *still* true. The conventional wisdom has always been that home ownership is better financially than renting, that renting is

Chart 12.1 ■ RENT OR BUY				
Purchase Price **Expenses:**	**Rent**	**$50,000** **Buy 1**	**$70,000** **Buy 2**	**$80,000** **Buy 3**
Mortgage or Rent Payment	$4,800	$4,177	$6,319	$8,424
Utilities	600	1,200	1,500	1,800
Property Taxes	0	800	900	1,000
Insurance	350	400	425	450
Repairs/Maintenance	0	250	300	350
Tax Savings	0	(1,000)	(1,500)	(2,000)
Total Annual Outflow	(5,750)	(5,827)	(7,944)	(10,024)
Gain:				
Appreciation (5%)	0	2,500	3,500	4,000
Interest Income (Net of Tax)	375	0	0	0
Effect on Net Worth	(5,375)	(3,327)	(4,444)	(5,524)
Effect on Net Worth after Sale with 7% Commission	0	(6,827)	(9,344)	(11,124)

• Based on $10,000 down; 10% interest rate mortgage; 25% tax rate.
• Appreciation is calculated at 5% of sales price.

simply "throwing money down the drain." That's generally been true since World War II because of three things: fixed-rate, long-term mortgages; appreciation (inflation); and the tax deductibility of mortgage interest. But let's look more closely at the numbers. Chart 12.1 compares a typical rent-versus-buy decision.

Note that the total annual outflow for paying rent of $400 per month is almost identical to that for purchasing a $50,000 house with a $10,000 down payment. The outflow for owning is actually slightly higher. As is usually the case, the home buyer is counting on appreciation in home values to make his decision a good investment. Assuming 5 percent annual appreciation on the $50,000 house, owning has a net cost of $3,327, whereas renting has a net cost of $5,375. If the house is sold at the end of the first year and a 7 percent real estate commission is paid, however, the net cost increases to $6,827, or almost $1,500 more than renting. If the house is sold after two years, the appreciation is such that you'd about break even compared to renting. The point is that if you can't plan on staying in a house for at least two years, you should seriously consider renting.

Obviously, there are a lot of variables in these calculations. The home appreciation rate may be higher or lower in your particular market. Selling the house yourself and avoiding a realtor's commission will have a big impact. And these figures don't take into account the front-end costs of buying (loan origination fees, appraisal fees, attorney fees, points, title insurance, etc.), all of which can add up to 2 to 3 percent of the loan amount. These costs must also be recovered in the appreciation of the residence. All in all, you need to live in a house at least two years before buying is clearly the best economic alternative. Once again, however, that assumes a fixed-rate mortgage and annual appreciation of at least 5 percent.

A house may be an investment, but a home is not.

One other common misconception is the belief that a home is a good investment. I have a strong reaction against that notion, because to those of us in the financial business, an investment is something you make for one of two purposes. You expect it to generate income, which a home does not do, or to appreciate enough in value that at some point you can sell it for a profit. But a home is rarely purchased with the idea of selling it when the value reaches a particular point.

A better way to state what most people mean is that a home may be a good purchase, but it's seldom bought with a true investment intent. I can assure you that most wives would be pretty upset if their husbands advised them that as soon as their home had appreciated 20 percent in value, it was going to be sold. This would be especially true if the wife had expended any time or emotional energy in redecorating and refurnishing the home. A house may be an investment, but a home is not. At best it's a good purchase.

In evaluating whether to take out a mortgage to buy a house rather than rent, we must go back to the decision-making rules from chapter 8 and apply them to this type of borrowing.

RULE 1: COMMON SENSE

Rule 1 says that the economic return from borrowing must be greater than the economic cost. That's just common sense. And because a home provides no economic return other than appreciation, the application of this rule comes down to determining whether the appreciation will be greater than the debt cost.

When money is borrowed for a home mortgage, the true cost of the interest must first be determined. Mortgage interest is deductible on federal and most state income tax returns, and it therefore costs the borrower less than the amount actually paid. Chart 12.2 illustrates the true cost of interest at different tax rates. In most cases, adding your state's income tax rate to the federal rate gives you the overall rate that should be used. For illustration purposes, I have used

Chart 12.2 ■ TRUE COST OF INTEREST						
	Mortgage Interest Rate					
Tax Rate	**6.0%**	**8.0%**	**10.0%**	**12.0%**	**14.0%**	**16.0%**
10.0%	5.4%	7.2%	9.0%	10.8%	12.6%	14.4%
20.0	4.8	6.4	8.0	9.6	11.2	12.8
30.0	4.2	5.6	7.0	8.4	9.8	11.2
40.0	3.6	4.8	6.0	7.2	8.4	9.6
50.0	3.0	4.0	5.0	6.0	7.0	8.0

increments of 10 percent in the tax rates and increments of 2 percent in the interest rate charged.

If you're in a total tax bracket of 30 percent and are considering a 10 percent home mortgage, your true cost of interest is 7 percent. To say it another way, the government, in effect, pays 30 percent of your interest cost by allowing you to deduct it from your taxable income. However, there's no way to recover the other 70 percent of every dollar of interest paid.

Chart 12.3 takes the illustration one more step and shows the appreciation that's required to break even on a home mortgage at different down-payment levels and interest rates. The left-hand column lists the loan value. (If you put 10 percent down on a home, you have a loan value of 90 percent.) Listed across the top are interest rates that might be charged by the lending insti-

Chart 12.3 ■ APPRECIATION REQUIRED TO BREAK EVEN: TRUE INTEREST COST AT 30% TAX RATE						
Loan % to Cost of Home	Loan Interest Rate					
	6.0%	8.0%	10.0%	12.0%	14.0%	16.0%
100.00%	4.20%	5.60%	7.00%	8.40%	9.80%	11.20%
90.00	3.78	5.04	6.30	7.56	8.82	10.08
80.00	3.36	4.48	5.60	6.72	7.84	8.96
70.00	2.94	3.92	4.90	5.88	6.86	7.84
60.00	2.52	3.36	4.20	5.04	5.88	6.72
50.00	2.10	2.80	3.50	4.20	4.90	5.60
40.00	1.68	2.24	2.80	3.36	3.92	4.48
30.00	1.26	1.68	2.10	2.52	2.94	3.36
20.00	0.84	1.12	1.40	1.68	1.96	2.24
10.00	0.42	0.56	0.70	0.84	0.98	1.12
0.00	0.00	0.00	0.00	0.00	0.00	0.00

tution, and below them are the true costs, assuming a 30 percent tax rate. Your true cost of mortgage interest will vary depending on your particular total state and federal tax rate.

Chart 12.4 is an illustration and application of the break-even computation. The chart assumes that a 30 percent taxpayer buys a home for $80,000 with a down payment of 20 percent.

Chart 12.4 ■ BREAK-EVEN ANALYSIS	
Assumptions:	
Tax Rate	30%
Home Cost (or Value)	$80,000
Down Payment (or Equity)	16,000
Loan Balance	64,000
Loan Interest Rate	8%
Appreciation Required to Break Even (chart 12.3)	4.48%
Proof:	
Interest cost—8% x $64,000	$5,120
Tax Reduction—$5,120 x 30%	(1,536)
True Annual Cost	$3,584
Appreciation Required to Break Even ($3,584/80,000)	4.48%

Conclusion:
This house must be worth $83,584 ($80,000 + 4.48%) at the end of the year for the appreciation to have offset the true interest cost of the mortgage. This does not include any closing cost that may have been incurred when the home was purchased. If two points were charged for closing cost, an additional $1,600 of appreciation must occur in the first year for you to break even.

The borrower must experience an appreciation of at least 4.48 percent in the first year in order to break even. Thus, a 4.48 percent or greater appreciation would be required to provide an

Chart 12.5 ■ PERSONAL BREAK-EVEN ANALYSIS	Your Situation	Example
Interest Rate on Loan	____% (A)	9.00%
Your Tax Rate (Total of Federal & State)	____% (B)	30.00%
True Interest Cost ([100%-B] x Interest Rate [A])	____% (C)	6.30%
Loan Percent of Value (Loan Balance/Home Value)	____% (D)	80.00%
Appreciation Required Next Year to Break Even (CxD)	____% (E)	5.04%
Your Home Cost or Value	$____ (F)	$80,000
Appreciation Needed to Break Even in Dollars (FxB)	$____ (G)	$ 4,032

In addition to the appreciation needed to cover the interest cost, appreciation is also needed to cover any sales or initial closing cost.

economic return greater than the economic cost.

Chart 12.5 provides blanks for you to fill in as you determine the appreciation you need to break even in your unique situation.

The implications for applying rule 1 to the borrowing decision for a home are as follows:

1. The greater the down payment and the lower the interest rate paid, the less appreciation needed to break even.

2. The lower the tax rate, the less advantageous it is to borrow on a home mortgage.

It's interesting that while these conclusions make clear, logical sense, "conventional wisdom" over the last several years contradicts them. The worldly view would be to put down as little money as possible in order to get the full benefit of leverage and inflation.

This analysis is applicable whatever the level of equity you have in your home. For example, if you've been paying on your mortgage for a number of years and now have a 60 percent equity in your home, just go down to the sixth line from the top in the left-hand column of chart 12.3, then read across to the column showing your interest rate, and you'll find the appreciation you need to continue to break even on your mortgage. Obviously, it's far less than someone who has only 10 percent equity in his home. The illustration will also work if you have an adjustable rate mortgage, where interest rates can change periodically. The assumptions still apply, and you can calculate for yourself, using chart 12.5, the appreciation you must have next year in order not to violate rule 1.

RULE 2: A GUARANTEED WAY TO REPAY

Rule 2 says that in borrowing, we should not presume upon the future, and thus there must be a guaranteed way to repay the loan. A home mortgage seemingly offers two guaranteed ways to repay. One is for the house itself to act as the collateral on the loan. The second is that the income being earned by the owner, or owners, provides the necessary money for the monthly payments.

In chapter 8, we reviewed exculpatory clauses in home mortgages. Such a clause provides a guaranteed way to repay. It's not the desirable way to repay, but it is a way.

Another way to repay using the home as collateral, but without an exculpatory clause, is to have so much equity in the house that there's almost no way the house could not be sold for the mortgage amount or more. If, for example, you had 60 percent equity in your home and you had to sell it as the only way to repay the mortgage, you could lower your price by more than 50 percent if necessary and still be able to pay off the loan. That's an extreme example, and I hope you never have to sell a house for half its value, but it shows the degree of loan protection provided by a high level of equity.

Without an exculpatory clause or significant equity in a home, your ability to make the monthly payments will depend on your stream of income, and there's almost no way to guarantee that income will continue. Illness, economic downturns, changes in family situation, and many other things make an income tenuous. If you have a good job with a good company, you may think your income is guaranteed, but it's not. Even if you are living off investment income, that's not guaranteed, either.

I stress this so strongly because many young couples borrow money for a home mortgage implicitly assuming that their income will, at the worst, remain constant. They generally don't even realize the risk they're taking.

The only way to determine the margin for error in taking on a home mortgage is to make a budget and live according to it. The risk won't go away entirely. However, the greater the margin for error in the budget, the more you have minimized the risk. And once again, the higher the down payment, the less the risk of losing the home because of a loss of income or a deflation in the home's value. Likewise, the lower the interest rate, the lower the risk.

RULE 3: PEACE OF HEART AND MIND

Rule 3 challenges you to examine your motives. The first questions that need to be addressed in making any major decision, and especially the decision to purchase a house, are, "Why do you want that particular house? What criteria are you using to evaluate the house? What motive is driving you? Is it to satisfy a need or a desire?"

If you're buying a house to meet a need for security or significance, the house has become your god. As pointed out earlier, only God can meet our real needs. If we try to use a house to meet those needs, we're dishonoring and disobeying God. In that case the decision should be, do not buy until your motives are pure.

The only way to discern whether you're violating any spiritual principles in deciding to borrow for a house is to spend time alone with the Lord, asking for His wisdom and guidance, which He has promised to provide.

Several years ago, I had been spending a considerable amount of time in my devotions asking the Lord what He would have us do in regard to our housing situation. As our children got older and bigger, our house got smaller and smaller. We wanted to move into a somewhat larger house for our children to grow up in, entertain in, and eventually come back to, along with spouses and grandchildren.

Periodically I read through the book of Proverbs, one chapter a day for a month. And on July 24, I read this in Proverbs 24:27: "Prepare your outside work, make it fit for yourself in the field; and afterward build your house." It was no coincidence, I'm sure, that the business I had started had matured to the point that it was operating successfully. I had spent a number of years bringing it to that stage. As my attention shifted to buying or building another house, this Scripture confirmed to me that the time was right for us to spend the emotional, mental, and financial resources necessary to move into another home.

Many times, God confirms the direction in which I'm headed. He uses other people, circumstances, or events, but most often I've found that He confirms or redirects decisions I'm in the process of making through His Word.

The other spiritual questions we addressed earlier were related to Colossians 3:15: "And let the peace of God rule in your hearts, to which also you were called in one body; and be thankful." As you make your mortgage decision, do you experience the peace of God ruling in your heart? Are you convinced you are acting in accordance with God's will? How do you know it's God speaking to you when you have that peace? I guess the best way to answer is that you'll *know* you know or you'll *know* you don't know. It's a matter of personal conviction by the Holy Spirit.

Many people are afraid to put their decisions before God because they assume He's a heavenly killjoy who doesn't want them to have anything good or desirable. That is not the God revealed in the Bible, however, and such an attitude is almost blasphemous. The proper attitude is to trust God to give you direction and provide for you.

Then ask yourself these questions:

1. Will my peer group give me the wisdom, discernment, and guidance I need?
2. Will the lender make sure I don't make a financial mistake?
3. Will the real estate agent guide me unerringly to buy no more house than I can afford?

God is the only One you can trust fully to provide for your unique and personal needs. There's risk associated with trusting Him (you may not always like His answers), but that's what faith is all about. Hebrews 11:8 praises Abraham's faith this way: "By faith Abraham obeyed when he was called to go out to the place which he would afterward receive as an inheritance. And he went out, not knowing where he was going." Risk depends on the object of your faith, and with God there is no risk, even though it feels like risk. If you're contemplating buying a house, I recommend you read Hebrews 11 several times to get into your mind and heart the truth that God can be trusted to guide you in this decision.

RULE 4: UNITY

In the book *Money and Marriage*, Russ Crosson suggests a question couples should ask themselves in making this decision. I paraphrase it as follows: "Which would make us more anxious, living in a smaller house and seeing our income go up enough to support a larger house, or living in a larger house where, if our income went down, we might not be able to afford the mortgage payments and so would run the risk of losing the house?" Asking yourselves that question is an excellent way to evaluate whether you're potentially making a foolish financial decision and risking your financial future.

One other point regarding unity for husbands and wives on this decision is that women typically have a lower tolerance for mortgage debt than men do. A woman's home is the center of her influence and her environment, and she knows instinctively that debt puts it at risk. A man views a home much differently. To him it's more a signal to the world of how well he's doing financially. As such, and because men are greater risk takers by nature anyway, he has a much higher debt tolerance than his wife. The partners should blend their needs to come to the right decision regarding a mortgage. No house is a home when the debt on it is a source of conflict.

I have applied this rule as it relates to the mortgage decision primarily to husbands and wives, because they're typically the ones making such a choice. But you may be a single person desiring to buy a house. My counsel is to follow these same rules, putting yourself in an accountability relationship with an older, wiser person to help you think through the decision. It will still be your decision, and you—not the other person—will live with the consequences. However, seeking the counsel of an elder is biblical and, consequently, wise.

SPECIFIC HOME MORTGAGE DECISIONS

Following the four basic borrowing rules in making the initial assessment of whether to take out a home mortgage is really only the beginning point in the decision-making process. If you think you should borrow, you have to deal with such questions as:

1. What type of mortgage should you get?
2. What term, or length of repayment terms, should you agree to?
3. Are home equity loans wise?
4. Is it advisable to pay off a mortgage early?
5. What about refinancing a mortgage during times of falling interest rates?
6. For young couples, what about equity sharing as a way to get into a home for the first time?
7. How should you view credit life insurance?

Let's answer each question in turn.

Type and Term of Mortgage

In trying to evaluate what type of mortgage to get, you'll have to learn many terms: ARMs, PLAMs, Fannie Maes, Freddie Macs, VA loans, buy downs, and so on. The variety in terminology is limited only by lenders' creativity. In addition, mortgage loans can be entered into for almost any number of years up to at least 30, and in some cases 50, years.

Addressing first the type of loan, I can safely say that anything other than a fixed-rate, fixed-term loan is an attempt to make it "easy" on the buyer and to protect the lender in the event of changed circumstances (i.e., rising interest rates). Therefore, ARMs (adjustable rate mortgages) and PLAMs (price level adjusted mortgages) are not wrong, just much riskier. The lender in each case is protected, and you, the buyer, are the one taking all the chances. You're implicitly assuming either deflation or an income rising with inflation.

If you're considering taking any type of adjustable mortgage, make sure it includes two things. First, there should be absolutely no possibility of negative amortization (where the amount you owe actually goes *up* rather than down) on the loan. Second, there should be caps on possible increases in the interest rate charged. For ARMs, that cap has typically been 5 or 6 percent over the life of the loan (1 or 2 percent per year), and I see no reason to ever agree to a higher total cap. The notion of "being able to afford it" by accepting a smaller payment at the beginning, but taking the risk of a larger payment or negative amortization later in the loan life, is an unnecessary risk and should not be taken. It is a deception and comes from a wrong motive.

In evaluating mortgages other than the fixed-rate, fixed-term type, *you should assume the payments are going to go up the maximum each year and do your planning accordingly*. Don't assume your income will go up proportionately. The safest way to plan for that type of mortgage is to assume your income is constant and your mortgage payments go up as much as possible each

Chart 12.6 ■ TIMES A HOME WILL BE PAID FOR USING A MORTGAGE TO PURCHASE							
Mortgage Term in Years	Loan Interest Rate						
	7.0%	8.0%	9.0%	10.0%	11.0%	12.0%	13.0%	14.0%
5	1.18	1.22	1.25	1.28	1.30	1.33	1.37	1.40
10	1.40	1.46	1.52	1.60	1.65	1.72	1.80	1.86
15	1.62	1.72	1.83	1.93	2.05	2.16	2.28	2.40
20	1.86	2.01	2.16	2.32	2.48	2.64	2.81	2.98
25	2.12	2.32	2.52	2.73	2.94	3.16	3.38	3.61
30	2.40	2.64	2.90	3.16	3.43	3.70	3.98	4.27

period. Then ask yourself, *Can we afford it?* If you follow these rules, you'll understand much better the risks associated with an adjustable mortgage.

The term of the loan is relatively easy to evaluate. Chart 12.6 indicates how many times you will pay back the original amount borrowed, assuming various interest rates and terms in years. For example, if you borrow money at a 14 percent rate on a 30-year mortgage, you will pay back 4.27 times the original amount borrowed. So the true cost of the home, ignoring the time value of money and the tax impact of the interest payments, is over four times what you thought you paid for it.

Notice what happens when you cut the

term of the mortgage in half, to 15 years, and leave the interest rate at 14 percent. Even though you borrow the same amount, you pay back only 2.4 times the original amount borrowed. Again this ignores the time value of money and the tax impact of the interest, which will change these calculations somewhat. But the conclusion is still clear that the shorter the term of the mortgage, the less you pay in interest.

Thus, my recommendations are simple regarding the type and term of the mortgage:

1. You're better off in the long run to use a fixed-rate mortgage rather than any type of adjustable loan. The latter almost always forces you to assume favorable economic circumstances in the future, and they may not in fact occur.

2. You should put down at least 20 percent when buying a house, even though it's possible to put down as little as 5 percent. Once again, the reason is to reduce the danger of presumption.

3. If at all possible, choose a 15-year loan instead of a 30-year loan. The payments are typically only 20 to 25 percent more per month, but the total amount paid over the life of the mortgage is significantly less.

I've been asked whether the fact that home mortgages are typically paid off in eight years (because the house is sold again) affects my recommendations, since they seem to assume a home buyer will be in the house long term. But whether you're in a house 3 years, 15 years, or 30 years makes no difference. The shortest-term loan at the lowest rate with the largest down payment is always the most prudent approach in mortgaging a house.

There's a significant risk in accepting an adjustable rate mortgage because you think you're only going to be in the home a few years. Such a loan is essentially a bet that the future will bring favorable economic conditions, and if those conditions don't come about, the borrower pays the price. Even with a 2 percent yearly cap on the interest rate, the monthly payment can go up dramatically. Unless income goes up just as dramatically, you may find yourself unable to make the payments.

Home Equity Loans

Home equity loans can be useful in certain circumstances; they can convert what would typically be nondeductible expenses into deductible expenses. They can also be useful in meeting short-term needs, such as for a college education. However, like any other form of debt, they're easy to enter into but deceptively difficult to pay off. The greatest danger with a home equity loan is that it risks a valuable asset, your home equity, for something less secure, such as an automobile, a vacation, or a boat.

In addition, home equity loans typically

have variable rates of interest, with no cap on how high the interest rate can go. Thus, when interest rates rise, these loans can be tremendously expensive to repay.

My recommendation is to use the four rules discussed earlier before deciding to obtain a home equity loan for any reason. Be extremely careful about entering into that form of debt, as it may become a real burden and put your house in jeopardy.

Early Mortgage Payoff

On occasion, perhaps through a windfall or through prudent, long-term savings, couples have an opportunity to pay off a mortgage early. It's surprising the number of times I'm asked about it. My answer is that it may not be as much an economic question as it is a peace-of-mind question. I typically respond by asking the couple to close their eyes and think about not having a home mortgage. Do they feel better about that alternative or about having the money in the bank? Almost always the answer is, "We have a greater sense of security when the mortgage is paid off." That may be more true for the wife than for the husband; if so, I always recommend they go ahead and pay the mortgage off.

There is no benefit from a tax standpoint of not paying off a mortgage. If you have a $100,000 mortgage costing 10 percent and a $100,000 investment earning 10 percent, you're earning and paying taxes on $10,000 and paying $10,000 of interest with the same tax impact. Therefore, it's a "wash" situation.

To look at the investment aspect of paying off the mortgage another way, assume a $50,000 mortgage at 10 percent, costing you $5,000 per year in interest. If you have a $50,000 investment fund, it must earn more than 10 percent *risk-free* just to be equivalent to paying off the mortgage. Otherwise, paying off the mortgage is the most desirable use for those funds. It's the same thing as a guaranteed, risk-free return, because you no longer have to pay out the amount of money you've been paying in interest.

The illustration from the last chapter showing the value of paying cash for a car is applicable here as well. The best alternative is to pay off the mortgage and then go on paying yourself (saving) an amount equal to the mortgage payments.

One other aspect of paying off a mortgage, however, is your need for liquidity (cash). If your need for liquidity is high, for whatever reason, it wouldn't be wise to pay off or even pay down the mortgage using all your liquid funds. Liquidity gives you flexibility to meet changing circumstances and emergencies. A couple should have at least three to six months of living expenses in an emergency fund before considering using excess funds to pay off the home mortgage.

Refinancing a Mortgage

When interest rates fall, people ask whether they should refinance their mortgages to lock in a lower interest rate. Generally, that's a wise move. However, the attorneys' fees, appraisal fees, points charged, and so on make it costly to refinance. A rule of thumb is that the new rate should be at least 2 percent less than the rate you're currently paying in order for the refinancing to make economic sense. Because the closing costs can be a total of 3 to 5 percent of the loan amount, it will usually take about two years to recoup those expenses at the 2 percent differential in rates. Therefore, one other consideration is that you should be planning on staying in the home for at least two more years.

Another consideration in refinancing is whether you have the freedom to do so without paying a prepayment penalty. By checking the loan document or calling the lender, you can determine your cost to refinance. It may very well be that you can negotiate those costs with the lender, even though the lender will be taking a lower interest rate (better that than have you borrow from someone else).

Equity Sharing

An article in the September 1987 issue of *Money* magazine reported the following: "The American middle-class is getting priced out of the housing market. Numbing house prices have become a fact of life in the Northeast, California, Washington D.C., Chicago, central North Carolina, and many other areas with booming economies or shortages of raw land. What is more, this year incomes are not rising nearly so much. Add to that the spike in mortgage rates in April and you have the most serious housing crunch in years.

"Consider the statistics: the median price of a new house, now a record $110,000, has risen 21% over the past year, while total personal income rose only 4%. Houses costing $200,000 or more now account for a record 13% of new home sales. As prices have headed higher, the national home ownership rate has fallen to its lowest level in 10 years; today only 64% of the adult population own their own houses, down from 66% in 1980. Seen another way, another 800,000 people would own homes if the ownership rate had remained at its 1980 level.

"Behind the figures are thousands of disappointed prospective home-buyers, most of whom make middle-class incomes of $30,000-$60,000 annually."

Even though those statistics are now several years old, they point out what happens to young families. They can be priced right out of the housing market even though their income is rising. This is especially true in heavily populated areas because of the scarcity of land.

As a result, many young couples are entering

into equity-sharing arrangements—someone else, often an investor, makes the down payment on the home in exchange for a share in the home's appreciation. There are many variations on how equity-sharing deals are structured. Who gets the tax deductions, how the appreciation is to be split, and who is liable for the mortgage can all be negotiated.

Because of the complexity of this type of arrangement and its applicability to such a small number of people, I'm not going to cover in detail how to structure such a deal. My recommendation, however, is that if equity sharing seems to make sense in your case, the terms need to be well understood by all parties concerned. And *without exception*, the terms should be reduced to writing and signed by all concerned, even if the arrangement is with a parent.

The terms of the equity-sharing relationship must give both parties an opportunity to get out of the deal at their singular option. This may require the sale of the home or a buyout of the other party. Such a sale may not be desirable to the people living in the home, but it's more desirable than continuing in a relationship that becomes antagonistic.

Credit Life Insurance
Credit life insurance is a policy offered when someone borrows money from a lending institution. In the event of the death of the insured

(borrower), the insurance company will pay off the mortgage, leaving the survivors with a debt-free home. A lender may make credit life insurance a requirement if the loan-to-value is greater than 80 percent. However, the lender can't require you to use any particular insurance company.

Most people entering into a mortgage have never considered purchasing life insurance to cover the value of the mortgage or the fact that they might be required to have it. Therefore, when it's offered by the lender, that seems an easy and fairly inexpensive way to obtain it.

Typically, however, credit life insurance is far more expensive than a comparable annual renewable term policy. And in some cases it may be 20 to 50 times higher than annual renewable term. Additionally, credit life insurance is for an amount that declines over time as the mortgage amount decreases, whereas annual renewable term insurance gives a fixed amount of coverage that does not decrease over time, even though the premiums may go up.

I recommend strongly that you obtain life insurance to cover a mortgage balance. In fact, a rule of thumb for all your life insurance needs would be to have a total amount adequate to (1) cover all debt, (2) provide a college education for children if that's a goal, (3) supply at least ten years' worth of current annual living expenses, and (4) meet any other special needs a family may have.

The kind of life insurance to get is the second important matter. Shop more than one company, much as you would for auto insurance. You'll learn a lot about the different kinds of insurance and the rates charged. More important, you'll no doubt save a considerable sum of money over the life of the mortgage by doing your own shopping and buying of life insurance rather than letting the lender do it for you.

One extra annual payment can reduce the total term of the mortgage by almost a third.

It's not at all unusual for that credit life insurance company to be owned by the lender, or for a large commission to be paid to the lender for placing that insurance. The lender is not offering you the credit life insurance as a benevolent gesture.

A FREE LUNCH

Earlier we did a comparison of mortgage terms, tax benefits, and interest rates to determine the true cost of a loan. We concluded that a shorter-term loan at a lower interest rate is the most advantageous way to purchase a home. We also determined that the lower the tax rate, the more this is true. Although the payments for a 15-year mortgage will be 20 to 25 percent more than those for a 30-year loan, they'll last only half as long.

In effect, the shorter mortgage is like a free lunch, because you're borrowing the same amount of money at the same interest rate but having to pay far less in total payments. Thus, the true cost of the home is significantly less than what it would be if you financed over a longer time period.

An alternative way to accomplish the same effect is to make one extra payment per year. Chart 12.7 shows the incredible impact of this strategy. That one extra annual payment can reduce the total term of the mortgage by almost a third.

There are several other ways to make early payments as well. You can pay one-half your usual monthly payment twice a month and

Chart 12.7 ■ EFFECT OF ONE EXTRA PAYMENT PER YEAR ON A 30-YEAR FIXED-INTEREST-RATE MORTGAGE						
Mortgage Int. Rate	Original No. of Paymts	Actual No. of Paymts	Differ- ence	Payment	Amount Saved	Actual No. of Years Paid
8.00%	360	279	81	$440.26	$35,661.06	23
10.00	360	257	103	526.54	54,233.62	21
12.00	360	235	125	617.17	77,146.25	19
14.00	360	213	147	710.92	104,505.24	17

reduce your interest costs. You can add one-twelfth of a payment to each payment and thereby end up with one extra payment per year. You can also make periodic lump-sum payments of principal.

Before doing any of these things, however, you need to check with the lender to determine that prepayments will be accepted. Ask also about rules regarding those prepayments. Some mortgage companies, for example, will use them to reduce the principal amount owed but not to reduce the payments; and if you're in default one payment in the future, you're in default on the mortgage. This is true even if you've prepaid a significant part of the principal amount borrowed.

The best alternative when prepaying the mortgage is to have the mortgage company commit to you that it will accept that prepayment in lieu of future payments. This will be critical should you ever find it necessary, because of extenuating circumstances, not to make a payment when it's due. Determining the lender's prepayment policy is best done before the mortgage is entered into, as there's no real incentive for the lender to change the terms of the loan once the documents are signed with terms in its favor.

SUMMARY

You need not understand all the buzzwords if you understand the principles underlying mortgages.

The fact of the matter is that the best mortgage is no mortgage. The second-best alternative is a fixed-rate, short-term mortgage. The third-best option is a fixed-rate, 30-year mortgage.

My last word of advice regarding home mortgages is to be willing to wait until you have accumulated at least a 20 percent down payment. Housing prices may inflate during your waiting, but God is sovereign, and He can still provide the housing you need when you need it. I would be very cautious about entering into any mortgage when you have less than 20 percent to put down. I would also recommend extreme caution when considering a home equity loan. In addition, remember that there's no sense in paying for credit life insurance through a lending institution when you can do much better yourself by shopping for an appropriate amount of life insurance.

CHAPTER THIRTEEN

Other Debt

The last two chapters have covered in detail the two types of borrowing that affect almost all Americans, installment debt and mortgage debt. However, I also receive many questions regarding other types of borrowing. So in this chapter I'm going to cover these five areas:

1. Borrowing for investments
2. Borrowing by businesses
3. Borrowing for a college education
4. Borrowing from life insurance policies
5. Borrowing by churches

The problem with discussing these areas is that most of them generate a high degree of emotion because of what they mean to the individual or group involved. The issue of borrowing to finance a new church building, for example, creates not only emotional energy, but also tremendous spiritual conviction.

In examining each type of borrowing, I'll use the four basic rules developed in chapter 8.

They provide some objectivity in evaluating these emotionally charged areas.

A decision can never be better than the alternatives considered.

The other problem with assessing these forms of debt is that they're less clear-cut than credit card or installment debt. Debt incurred for every investment, every business opportunity, every church building program, and every college education appears economically wise and certain to have a way of repayment. What we need to do, then, is look more closely to see if in fact these types of borrowing meet the four rules; and if they do, we'll want to think about the assumptions that conclusion is based on.

INVESTMENT DEBT

We examined investment debt using the four rules back in chapter 8. One point that needs to be reemphasized here, however, is that no investment looks bad initially—investments "just happen" to "go bad." And because all investments are "good deals," there's a tremendous temptation to assume it makes economic sense to borrow money to enter into an investment.

With every investment looking like a good deal initially, the decision maker is easily lured into a "binary trap." A binary trap sets one up to ask, "Should I do this or not?" It assumes those are the only two options, thus begging the real question, which is, "What's the best use for the money I have?"

A decision can never be better than the alternatives considered. When making an investment decision, if you consider only whether or not to make that particular investment, you're ignoring all the other alternative uses for that money, which may very well have a higher priority and be of greater value to you. The best way to avoid the binary trap is to ask yourself, *Are there any other possible uses for this money?*

One other issue regarding investment debt is a particular kind of investment that requires a payment over several years before the investment is fully made. This is typically called a "multiple pay" investment. The question is whether such an investment is really debt.

To answer that question, let me ask, "Do you make an agreement to pay additional amounts in future years?" If you do, you have entered into a debt contract. It's that simple. Therefore, it needs to be evaluated in the same way as other types of borrowing. It must meet the four rules. And the only way this type of investment can meet rule 2 (a guaranteed way to repay) is for you either to set aside the money to make the payment or to have the lender agree that *at your option* you can return the investment to him as full payment for the debt. I might add that I have never seen a lender agree to do that.

A final caution regarding investment borrowing: Most people should never consider borrowing for investments—or even make investments, for that matter—until they're totally out of debt, including mortgage debt. Whenever extra cash flow is available that could be used for an investment debt payment, it should be used to pay off all other forms of existing debt. Repaying existing debt gives you a *guaranteed* investment return.

BUSINESS DEBT

Business debt looks a lot like investment debt and should be evaluated similarly. Business borrowing *always* appears to be a good deal. Most new businesses don't have enough capital with which to start, so they quickly run into the need to borrow. Such debt certainly seems to meet at least the first rule of borrowing, and the other rules seem to be of less consequence when the first is so overwhelmingly met. The return on the moneys borrowed seems to be so significant that there's no question about repayment. The spiritual convictions, along with the unity rule, are ignored because the deal appears to be "so right."

The way to avoid the undercapitalization problem in a new business is to make sure there's a well-prepared and well-reviewed business plan in place before the business is begun.

My general counsel is to calculate the amount of start-up money needed and then double it. Using that figure, you might come close to the amount of capital actually used.

In my own business, we have needed almost six times the original capital projection, which fortunately we have been able to fund without borrowing. We needed so much money for a reason typical to new businesses: success. The additional capital is required to fund a buildup in receivables, inventory, marketing costs, and so on. In fact, working capital is the greatest need of a prospering business, and the strong temptation will be to borrow that capital instead of saving it ahead of time or bringing in other investors.

> *The Christian has a moral obligation to repay every amount owed whether or not he is personally liable for it.*

One question I'm frequently asked regarding business debt is related to rule 2, a guaranteed way to repay. Because a corporate form of organization limits the liability of the shareholders to their invested dollars, many times a businessperson will assume that business debt is OK. The businessman himself takes on no personal legal liability for the firm's debts.

My belief, however, is that in a closely held business, the lenders are looking to the owner to be responsible for the debt, even though they don't require personal liability. And I believe the Christian has a moral obligation to repay every amount owed whether or not he is personally liable for it.

I recently had the unpleasant experience of observing a Christian businessman borrow his way into bankruptcy. Because he had organized his company as a corporation, he was able to walk away from the debts he had generated. But by doing that, he acquired a terrible reputation, not only for himself, but for the whole Christian community as well. A legitimate question was asked by the town's non-Christians: "Is this the way Christians do business?" I cannot say it any more plainly than to quote Psalm 37:21: "The wicked borrows and does not pay back." You can't hide behind legalities when borrowing money. It is the responsibility of the one who entered into the debt to repay it *regardless of his legal protection*.

COLLEGE LOANS

According to the *Journal of Accountancy* (March 1989), "The cost of sending a child to a private university for four years now averages more than $50,000, while the cost of a four year public university education averages $18,000. By the

year 2007, the Department of Education esti-
mates the total cost to attend a private university will increase to $200,000, and to $60,000 for
a public university. These statistics cited last
year by a Treasury Department official testifying
before the Senate Finance Committee spotlight a
major financial problem facing parents: how to
pay for their children's college costs."

The prognosis for college costs is so bad that
if there are two children in a family and both of
them go to private schools, the parents are likely
to spend as much for four-year college educa-
tions as they would to purchase a home—and
that doesn't allow for any graduate schooling.
That expense is especially burdensome because
it's compressed into four years as opposed to a
30-year mortgage for the purchase of a home.

The problem of funding a college education
may not fall on the parents, however. Maybe the
child has chosen to pay his own way through
college, or perhaps his parents just can't afford
to send him. But that doesn't mean a secondary
education is out of the question.

Many years ago, I counseled with a prospective seminary student who really felt God was
calling him to full-time ministry. But he didn't
have the money. His question to me at the time
was whether he should borrow the money. A
problem with borrowing to go to seminary, however, is that the salary earned after graduation
may never be sufficient to repay the loan. I

advised him that if he was sure God had called him to go to seminary, he should forget borrowing and take one day and one semester at a time, trusting that God would meet his needs from His resources, because it didn't look as if he would ever have a guaranteed way to repay a loan.

I received the following letter from that young man. It makes the point better than I can that God is faithful to meet the needs of those who depend on Him.

Dear Mr. Blue:

I am sure you may not remember me as I have only met you via the telephone on the VOX POP radio program. My question to you went something like this . . . "I'm single, age 36, no outstanding debts (which you said was un-American!), and I have a small savings account (around $600). I dislike going into debt. I'm feeling called to the ministry. Should I borrow money to enroll in seminary?" Your response to me was something to the effect that I should not limit God, but to step out and trust Him to supply the money. I did just that, and the blessings have been phenomenal. May I share with you what has happened? On my first day of summer Greek I received a note in my mailbox saying an anonymous donor had sent a check to my account for $325; four weeks later, another note, and another $325. My thoughts were that someone had just wanted me to get a good start in seminary, so I thought nothing of it until a third check arrived in early September for $375. I was then notified by the Financial Aid Office that the checks would apparently be coming each month for the foreseeable future, and they have, ranging from $325 to $475.

This is not the end, however! In late August, following the summer session, I went to visit a friend, and helped paint a house for a week. I never expected to be paid, but he insisted, and I received a check for $180.

The church where I was raised (I am no longer a member there) sent me a letter and a check for $300, saying they had decided to give me part of the mission budget. In October I knew I was to be the recipient of the Sunday school mission offering; I expected $30 to $40. They decided to open it up to anyone in the church who wanted to give, and I received a check for $376.50.

In November I was able to preach at that church. During the service, the pastor announced that an offering plate would be placed at the back door for anyone wanting to assist me financially; the offering was $406.

My work-study position here at the seminary is in the Advancement and Development Office, and because of a shortage of help in January, I was given the opportunity to work extra hours. And then last week I was asked to work additional hours during a minister's conference on campus.

The Lord knows I came here on faith, and He has supplied "above and beyond all that I could ask or think." My goal is to be a hospital chaplain, and I am excited about what God has in store for me.

May God continue to bless your work.

I Samuel 12:24 (RSV)

Please understand I'm not suggesting that borrowing to go to college is wrong per se—no more than I've suggested getting a home mortgage is wrong. But the proper way to evaluate a college loan is the same way we've evaluated every other borrowing decision, using the four basic rules.

If you determine that borrowing to pay for a college education meets the rules and you are not denying God an opportunity to work, my challenge to you is that immediately upon graduation, you establish repaying the debt as your top financial priority. The federal government has found that because it makes or subsidizes most student loans, many students don't feel a moral obligation to repay their loans, even though they have well-paying jobs. The Christian, however, has no option to ignore his obligations.

Before borrowing any money, you should ask, "Are there any alternatives?" In the case of funding a college education, there *are* some alternatives to consider. The absolute best alternative is to begin early to save for it. For example, if you deposit $100 per month for 18 years in a fund earning 12 percent per year, that fund will grow to $75,786. A one-time deposit of $5,000 would grow to $42,893 over the same time period. Thus, starting early to save for a college education greatly reduces the burden on the family budget when Junior actually goes off to school.

Many stock mutual funds offer systematic investment programs in which your bank account can be drafted each month for a set amount. This amount can be as low as $50, depending on the fund. If you start right away and have a 10-to-18-year time horizon (depending on your child's age), you'll be able to weather the ups and downs of different market cycles. Many funds have exceeded a 12 percent annual return over a long time period.

In addition to your own savings, it may be helpful to have your children save a certain percentage of the money they earn and receive as gifts for birthdays and holidays. With a small amount here and there, some discipline, and a long-term perspective, significant amounts can be accumulated toward college expenses.

A third alternative is to require that your children earn all or part of their own way through school. They can take summer jobs, work for a couple of years prior to college, work while in school, and so on. Many parents seem to think they owe their children a college education. But it should be considered a luxury rather than a necessity. Just because your kids' peers are attending college on a full ride from their parents doesn't mean that's also your responsibility.

Perhaps God has a better plan for your children than sending them to college, or maybe they should work their way through. I would never recommend borrowing to fund a college education for a child who was unwilling to act responsibly toward the opportunity. That may mean providing a portion of the cost, and it certainly means maintaining good academic performance.

Another alternative is a tuition prepayment program. The parents prepay a child's tuition at a particular school based on current costs. The school invests the money and guarantees the payment of tuition costs when the child reaches college age. Obviously, the earlier that prepayment is made, the less the initial cost to the parents.

The big disadvantage is that the child may not want to matriculate at the school the parents chose years earlier. Another risk is that college costs won't continue to escalate, since the purpose of the program is to protect against rising costs. If costs stay level or drop, paying into such a plan will prove to be an unwise decision. The better approach is to put a "prepayment" in your own savings program and allow that money to grow at compounded rates of return. If costs should drop, the excess in the fund is yours.

There are many options for saving ahead of time. For example, you could use Series EE savings bonds, which offer tax-free accrual of interest. Beginning in 1990 (and depending on the parents' level of income), the accumulated interest will also be tax exempt if the bond is redeemed to pay the higher education expenses of parents or children.

The use of the Unified Gift to Minors Act is another, though less attractive, approach to saving. It offers two advantages. First, even though all the earnings are taxed, they're taxed at the child's lower rate until the child reaches age 14. Second, the account does set the money aside toward that future, worthwhile goal.

Investing in zero coupon bonds is yet

another way to save for college education. While taxed on the growth in value each year (with no income actually received), they're a convenient forced savings plan, because the decision to buy them needs to be made only once. After that, nothing is required except to pay the taxes each year and redeem them at maturity for the full face amount.

Because many children's investments are now taxed at the parents' rate, nontaxable investments such as municipal bonds have become more attractive. Another traditional vehicle for providing for a child's college education is the cash value in whole-life life insurance. Buying a whole-life policy on a child at birth is inexpensive and makes for forced periodic savings that can be used when the child reaches college age. Another insurance product is a single-premium, cash-value policy, which for a child at birth could cost $20,000 and be worth $65,000 by age 18.

When considering any cash-value life insurance product, it's worthwhile to shop around and buy from a company that has a history of increasing its dividends to policyholders as interest rates rise.

Still other vehicles, such as trusts, can be used to set aside money for college education. This book is not designed to provide a detailed explanation of all the alternatives. Just remember to start early and save ahead of time. Your choice of method isn't nearly as important as the decision to be disciplined to save. By saving, you reduce the need to consider whether a college loan is desirable.

LIFE INSURANCE LOANS

Money borrowed from a whole-life insurance policy is called a life insurance loan. However, it isn't really debt. It's money you have accumulated as a sort of savings in a life insurance product, and it's yours any time you choose to cancel the policy. When you borrow, you're required to pay interest on the amount borrowed at a rate set in the insurance contract. The rate can be very low for older policies and fairly high and variable for new policies.

Even though the interest is no longer fully tax-deductible (as it used to be), you should consider this source of borrowing if you need a loan. You're effectively borrowing from yourself, and there's a guaranteed way of repayment—when you die (a guaranteed event, I'm afraid), the amount borrowed and not yet repaid (if any) will be repaid from the proceeds of the policy. If you used the money borrowed to purchase something that meets rule 1, you haven't effectively decreased your estate value. You've moved money from insurance cash value to another asset.

I'm frequently asked whether life insurance loans should be repaid, seeing that they don't have to be. The answer isn't easy, because the biggest variable is the insurance company itself. If it's a quality company that has a history of increasing dividends (which are really returns of excess premiums) to policyholders, repaying the loan can reduce your interest cost each year and also allow for a good, tax-free buildup of cash within the policy. In other words, it can be an excellent investment if your insurance is with a strong company.

The financial explanation of why repaying a life insurance loan may be a good investment is as follows: Assume you have a money market account earning 9 percent interest, and assume the dividend rate on a life insurance policy is also 9 percent. The interest earned in the money market fund is fully taxable, whereas the insurance dividends are tax-deferred and maybe even tax-free. Therefore, you have compounding working on a greater amount within the insurance policy than within the money market fund. And the insurance cash value is almost as easily available to you as funds in a money market account.

I'm not saying you should buy whole-life insurance as an investment or as a source from which to borrow. How to choose the right kind of insurance is a whole other subject that I addressed in my first book. What I am saying is that if you've borrowed money from a life insurance policy, it may make good sense to repay the loan as an investment. Additionally, if you have a whole-life policy and need to borrow money for whatever purpose, such a policy is typically a good place to get it. It's certainly better than a home equity or installment loan.

CHURCH DEBT

Church borrowing is a form of debt I think must be addressed in any book on debt, but I can promise you I don't look forward to addressing it because of the strong feelings for and against it. I'll do my best, though, to be clear and candid.

I once received a phone call from a full-time Christian worker who's also a good friend; he wanted my advice on whether he should invest in some bonds offered by his church. They were being offered to the congregation with a yield of 12 percent and in $5,000 increments. His question illustrates some of the problems I see in the whole area of church debt.

First, the church leadership was selling to its congregation the idea that these bonds were an investment and that the interest rate on them was attractive compared to other investments. If they truly were an investment, they should be evaluated as such and not as a charitable gift. So let's look at them from that standpoint.

An investment that is nonliquid (meaning it cannot be converted to cash readily) is always a higher-risk investment than something liquid, such as a money market fund, a

Treasury bill, or a certificate of deposit. Therefore, from an investment standpoint, a church bond has one strike against it, because it's very nonliquid.

A second strike against a church bond is the source of repayment. The church bond depends on the congregation's continuing to grow, or give, as it has in the past. But many things affecting a church can change (the pastor leaves, the surrounding neighborhood deteriorates, the economy turns down), making the repayment of that bond more risky than many other forms of investment.

Again, let me clarify: I have *not* said a church bond is a bad investment. I have said that if it's marketed and sold as an investment, it must be evaluated as such. And in that light, it is both nonliquid and much riskier than some investment alternatives. Because of the higher risk, the seller must compensate by paying a higher interest rate.

From the church's standpoint, the people are committing themselves to pay a premium interest rate to attract funds to the building program. This seems to fly right in the face of all I know about our God. The implicit assumption is that God is unable to provide the money, except at a premium interest rate, for facilities for His people.

I've heard most of the arguments for why church bonds make sense as a way to finance a building program. It's said that they're no different from any other form of mortgage and that the building acts as collateral for the amounts borrowed. It's also argued that they're the "only way" to provide for the expansion of facilities needed for the congregation to grow, which in turn will allow the ministry to take place.

Church bonds and a mortgage on a church building are legitimate forms of debt when you apply the rules. However, any mortgage presumes upon the future. And the way to avoid presuming upon the future is to have a guaranteed way to repay. If the lenders, be they the church congregation or a lending institution, will exculpate the church from any liability other than the collateral, the church has not violated that rule.

My real concern, however, is not whether church bonds are a traditional form of borrowing or even a "right" way to borrow, but whether they deny God an opportunity to work. Our family once belonged to a church in Atlanta that years ago made the commitment never to borrow to buy any property, build any buildings, or fund any programs. There has never been a lack of funds to do God's work in that church, and the congregation has continued to grow. It is now ministering to literally millions around the world. As someone once said, "God's work done in God's way will never lack God's resources."

I would strongly challenge any church's leaders to think seriously about the spiritual implications of borrowing money to fund God's programs. Are you sending a message to the world that God is unable to meet the needs of the church body? Are you sending a message to your own congregation that debt is an acceptable and even preferable way of meeting needs?

Ask yourselves the same questions individuals should ask themselves regarding rule 3: "Why are we borrowing money? What's the real motive?" Is your motive truly to be 100 percent obedient to our Lord in performing His work? If so, as I have challenged individuals, I would challenge you with Philippians 4:19: "And my God shall supply all your need according to His riches in glory by Christ Jesus." As Christians, we are called to be "salt and light." That doesn't mean we arrange better terms of financing; it means we operate *differently* from the way the world operates.

CONCLUSION

In this chapter we've looked at many types of borrowing, but we've continually come back to the same rules: (1) Does it make economic sense? (2) Do you have a guaranteed way to repay? (3) What are your spiritual convictions regarding this borrowing? (4) Is there unity with either your spouse or your accountability partner regarding the debt?

These rules will stand you in good stead with every borrowing decision if you'll take the time to evaluate the borrowing opportunity honestly in their light. No financial decision needs to be made so quickly that you can't take the time for this evaluation.

You don't need to be a banker to understand debt, credit, and borrowing. Romans 11:33-36 proclaims, "Oh, the depth of the riches both of the wisdom and knowledge of God! How unsearchable are His judgments and His ways past finding out! 'For who has known the mind of the LORD? Or who has become His counselor? Or who has first given to Him and it shall be repaid to him?' For of Him and through Him and to Him are all things, to whom be glory forever. Amen." God is the source of wisdom. Follow the four biblically based rules in evaluating debt and you'll avoid serious financial mistakes. More significantly, you'll avoid serious spiritual mistakes.

God desires His best for us and has given His best: our Lord Jesus Christ. How can we put anyone, especially a lender, in His place?

My final challenge is threefold. When contemplating a borrowing decision, ask yourself:

1. Have I considered every other alternative?
2. Does God have a better way?
3. Am I teaching my children and grandchildren the proper use of credit and debt?

My prayer is that the body of Christ will be *different* in a world that desperately needs to see an alternative to hedonistic, materialistic philosophies. Properly evaluating the use of debt and avoiding its misuse are ways we can demonstrate that our God is sufficient.

The ABCs of Salvation

Many people are troubled when they realize how simple it is to become a Christian. Some feel a need to make the gospel more difficult; others can't believe that God's plan of salvation is true. What does the Bible say?

ADMIT you are a sinner and cannot save yourself. First John 1:9 tells us to "confess our sins," to agree with God that we are sinners and need to be saved. This humbling before a holy God is necessary to understand what Christ did by dying for our sins.

BELIEVE what the Bible says about Jesus Christ. Do you believe that He is the Messiah and your only Savior? Do you believe He rose from the dead, ascended to heaven, and will come again? Your faith must be in what the Bible says about Jesus, not in your personal feelings or in your works. "Without faith it is impossible to please Him, for he who comes to God

must believe that He is, and that He is a
rewarder of those who diligently seek Him"
(Heb. 11:6). Through faith we express confi-
dence in what the Bible says about Jesus Christ.

COMMIT your life and future to Jesus
Christ. You can practice faith all your life
and yet fail to make a personal commitment to
Jesus. Have you made this commitment? If not,
why not do it now! The words are not important; God waits to hear your prayer of confes-
sion and commitment, a simple prayer like this:

"Lord, I confess that I am a sinner. I believe
that Jesus Christ paid for all my sins when He
died on the cross. I believe He rose from the
dead, ascended to heaven, and will one day
come again. I now commit my life to Him, trusting Him alone as my Savior. Thank You for lov-
ing me and saving me. In Jesus' name. Amen."

Then, if you've made that commitment to
Christ, find fellowship with His people by
attending a good, Bible-teaching church that
helps you to grow spiritually and to serve God.

Where to Get Help

If you need professional help in getting out of debt, there are several options. Our firm, Ronald Blue & Co., isn't really a debt-counseling agency. We're a financial planning firm helping individuals arrange their estates, investments, taxes, and giving. What debt counseling we do is almost always associated with planning for the use of *excess* cash flow rather than negative cash flows. If you need financial planning help, you can contact our office in Atlanta at 1-800-987-2987. But if your need is strictly to get out of debt, there are other, better places for that type of assistance.

DEBT COUNSELING RESOURCES

The first place to seek out debt counseling is your local church. Even if there is not a specific debt-counseling ministry, someone on the church staff should know where to send people for help. Debt problems are a common difficulty, confronted regularly by counselors.

Christian Financial Concepts (www.cfcministry.org, or 1-800-722-1976), founded by Larry Burkett, is a ministry with an extensive network of debt counselors all over the country and numerous educational resources on money management.

NFCC, The National Foundation for Consumer Credit (www.nfcc.org, or 1-800-388-CCCS) is another sound source for debt counseling. Although NFCC is not Christian-based, it can provide practical information and assistance.

FINANCIAL PLANNING RESOURCES

Ronald Blue & Co., LLC (www.ronblue.com, or 1-800-987-2987), founded in 1979 by the author, provides services based on biblical principles of financial management, including comprehensive, fee-only financial and estate planning, investment analysis and management, strategies for charitable giving, as well as complete tax preparation and business services for individuals and organizations.

BIBLE STUDY RESOURCES

Ronald Blue & Co., LLC (www.ronblue.com, or 1-800-987-2987) also has several educational resources available on money management from a biblical perspective, including the video training series *Master Your Money*.

Crown Ministries (www.crown.org, or 407-331-6000) has developed outstanding study materials for all ages on the biblical approach to stewardship and money management.

Other Books to Strengthen Your Relationships
From Focus on the Family®

Parents Guide to Top 10 Dangers Teens Face
Parents can help guard their teens against alcoholism, drug addiction, promiscuity and other reckless behaviors by reading Stephen Arterburn's *Parents Guide to Top 10 Dangers Teens Face*. Filled with proven principles, it helps parents heed the warning signs, ward off potential problems and direct their kids down the road to success. Paperback.

Give Them Wings
When kids hit their teenage years, the role of parents begins to change. In *Give Them Wings*, author Carol Kuykendall offers encouragement for raising kids to be responsible, godly men and women and for looking toward the empty nest with hope. Paperback.

Once a Parent, Always a Parent
Kids grow up, but they're still your kids! Steven Bly in *Once a Parent, Always a Parent*, shares practical ways to become involved—but not over-involved— in your adult child's life. Learn how to best provide support, encouragement, financial assistance, childcare and much more whether your child lives across the country or across the hall. Paperback.

Look for these special books in your Christian bookstore or request a copy by calling 1-800-A-FAMILY (1-800-232-6459). Friends in Canada may write Focus on the Family, P.O. Box 9800, Stn. Terminal, Vancouver, B.C. V6B 4G3 or call 1-800-661-9800.

Visit our Web site (www.family.org) to learn more about the ministry or to find out if there is a Focus on the Family office in your country.

FOCUS ON THE FAMILY®
Welcome to the family!

Whether you purchased this book, borrowed it, or received it as a gift, we're glad you're reading it. It's just one of the many helpful, encouraging, and biblically based resources produced by Focus on the Family for people in all stages of life.

Focus began in 1977 with the vision of one man, Dr. James Dobson, a licensed psychologist and author of numerous best-selling books on marriage, parenting, and family. Alarmed by the societal, political, and economic pressures that were threatening the existence of the American family, Dr. Dobson founded Focus on the Family with one employee and a once-a-week radio broadcast aired on 36 stations.

Now an international organization reaching millions of people daily, Focus on the Family is dedicated to preserving values and strengthening and encouraging families through the life-changing message of Jesus Christ.

Focus on the Family Magazines

These faith-building, character developing publications address the interests, issues, concerns, and challenges faced by every member of your family from preschool through the senior years.

Citizen
U.S. news issues

Clubhouse Jr.
Ages 4 to 8

Clubhouse
Ages 8 to 12

Breakaway
Teen guys

Brio
Teen girls
13 to 15

Brio & Beyond
Teen girls
16 to 19

Plugged In
Reviews movies,
music, TV

Enjoy the Rewards of Parenting with Focus on Your Child®

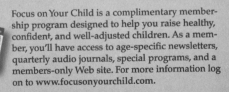

Focus on Your Child is a complimentary membership program designed to help you raise healthy, confident, and well-adjusted children. As a member, you'll have access to age-specific newsletters, quarterly audio journals, special programs, and a members-only Web site. For more information log on to www.focusonyourchild.com.

> **FOR MORE INFORMATION**

Online:
Log on to www.family.org

Phone:
Call toll free: (800) A-FAMILY

Find Guidance
for Your Family

Healing the Hurt in Your Marriage
Habitual avoidance of conflict is the #1 predictor
of divorce. But couples often avoid resolving their
differences because they don't know how to deal
with conflict effectively. *Healing the Hurt in Your
Marriage*, an updated repackage of Dr. Rosberg's *Do-
It-Yourself Relationship Mender*, provides a practical
step-by-step process for healthy resolution that heals
hurts and promotes forgiveness. (Paperback)

Give Them Wings
What can moms and dads do to prepare their kids
for life as responsible young adults and themselves for
the empty nest? *Give Them Wings* provides practical
insights to help their teens choose the right college,
embark on a career, and more. Best of all, it allows
parents the freedom to look toward the future with
hope. (Paperback)

Parents Guide to Top 10 Dangers Teens Face
As the teenage years approach, many parents feel
overwhelmed by the possible problems facing their
kids: premarital sex, drug use, eating disorders, and
pornography, to name a few. *Parents Guide to Top
10 Dangers Teens Face* will help you recognize a
developing problem and teach you how to combat
it. Previously released as *Steering Them Straight*.
(Paperback)